Praise for A Mother Apart

"An indispensable guide for mothers living without their children: profound, compassionate, realistic, hopeful and creative. A wonderful source for healing and reparation, it holds the wisdom of one who has come through this unique and rarely understood trauma. I wish it had existed years ago."

Rosie Jackson author of *Mothers Who Leave*

"In this touching, inspiring and deeply wise book, Sarah Hart has distilled the wisdom of her extensive personal and professional experience. It is a book to treasure, to return to again and again as compassion, insight and useful practical suggestions leap off every page. Sarah covers all the struggles and heartaches mothers in this situation are likely to encounter and shows us how to reach a deeper healing and love than we might ever have imagined possible. I am delighted such a beautiful book has been written at last about such a painful and frequently misjudged subject and wholeheartedly recommend it to anyone interested in the challenges of love, especially mothers, and most of all to those who love their children from afar."

Anne Geraghty author of *In the Dark and Still Moving*

"If you are a woman living apart from your children, take this book as your companion on the lumpy, bumpy journey toward a healthier life. Much more than a self-help book, Mothers Apart is rich with insight, compassion and a practical focused plan for developing different patterns of self care. This book is also a superb resource for the practitioner who supports the growing and diverse range of non-resident mothers eager to write their healing stories."

Diana L. Gustafson, Associate Professor, Faculty of Medicine, Memorial University

"*A Mother Apart* is an accessible and supportive guide for women who, for whatever reason, no longer have full-time residence of their children. In a thought provoking first chapter, Sarah Hart examines the stereotypical role of mother as primary carer which, despite changes in the position of women in society, continues to cause feelings of guilt and shame in mothers living apart from their children. She effectively dispels the myth that such mothers are selfish or inadequate and explains, on both an emotional and a practical level, how a mother can cope with the implications of living apart from her child. From the perspective of a family lawyer, there are particularly useful chapters in the book on how mothers can deal with the challenges of co-parenting with ex-partners, the impact of a new wife and "mother" figure in the child's life, how to help children cope with divorce and separation and how to make the most of contact when it takes place. I would highly recommend this book to mothers with shared residence or non-resident mothers whether or not they presently have contact with their children."

Miranda Fisher, Solicitor, Charles Russell LLP

"A much-needed perspective for women who are re-examining their roles and responsibilities as mothers."

Maria Housden author of *Hannah's Gift* and *Unravelled*

"A thoughtful and sensitive guide to a difficult issue."

Psychologies

A Mother apart

How to
**let go of guilt
& find happiness
living apart from
your child**

Crown House Publishing Limited
www.crownhouse.co.uk
www.chpus.com

Crown House Publishing Ltd
Crown Buildings, Bancyfelin, Carmarthen, Wales, SA33 5ND, UK
www.crownhouse.co.uk
and
Crown House Publishing Company LLC
6 Trowbridge Drive, Suite 5, Bethel, CT 06801, USA
www.chpus.com

British Library of Cataloguing-in-Publication Data
A catalogue entry for this book is available from the British Library.

13-digit ISBN 978-184590094-6
10-digit ISBN 184590094-4
LCCN 2007938978

The extract on page 3 has been reproduced with the kind permission of Hawthorn Press.
The quote on page 57 is reproduced with the kind permission of The Elizabeth Kübler Ross Foundation.
The author and the publisher gratefully acknowledge the permission granted to reproduce the copyright
material in this book.
Every effort has been made to trace copyright holders and to obtain their permission for the use of
copyright material. The publisher apologises for any errors or omissions and would be grateful if notified
of any corrections that should be incorporated in future editions or reprints of this book.

The names of women who shared their experiences in this book
have been changed to protect their privacy.

Contents

To my daughter Roxane

with deep love.

I would have dedicated this book to you
even if you hadn't asked me to,
but it means the world to me that you did.

Acknowledgements

I would like to say a wholehearted thank you to the mothers apart who have shared both good and tough times with me, over the years.

A very big thank you to the women who contributed their stories to this book—I know what it took for you to do so.

Thanks especially to …

Penny Cross for writing the Foreword and whose own book kept me company while I wrote this one, and Caroline Lenton and Beverley Randell at Crown House Publishing for championing this book and having confidence in me.

I would also like to thank …

All my friends who have supported me over the years, through the bites of lions and the nibbles of rabbits.

Joan Massella, my 'mominafrica', who has been my friend and source of instant moral fibre for twenty-two years.

Sue Jarvis for writing to me when I first discovered MATCH and latterly for long talks as I walk in the woods.

Anne Geraghty, my teacher, who inspires and mirrors the deep in me.

Pam Emery for the relief of many a blah-blah.

My father Reg, sisters Felicity and Roberta for having faith in me and Richard for his design ideas.

To my son Brett for his steadfast love, support, youthful energy and music. You are my joy.

Finally, to my partner Simon who has shown me how to climb mountains, observe the oneness in nature and see the wonder in even the tiniest of wild flowers. Your unfailing belief in me is a dream come true.

Foreword – Penny Cross

Chair of the charity MATCH (Mothers Apart from their Children)

This is a book for women with deep, hidden scars who may have been searching, intentionally or unconsciously, for help in healing them. This is also a book for therapists, counsellors, general practitioners, health practitioners and others looking to help such women. Look no further. You'll find it within this compellingly written self-help book underpinned by a profound compassion for, and deep understanding of, all mothers apart from their children across a wide range of circumstances. The impetus for this book came about because of Sarah Hart's own painfully acquired personal experience as a mother apart which later impelled her to acquire impressive professional and academic qualifications.

Sarah's eminently practical, therapeutic advice reflects an astonishing depth of feeling for mothers apart. Her deeply loving, tender approach will help to begin a journey back to happiness and one that people might not believe could ever take place. It will not be easy but it will not be lonely with Sarah to guide you each step of the way. If you ever doubted you'd 'find happiness living apart from your child', read Sarah's dynamic and positive approach to re-evaluating and re-thinking your life.

I wish I'd had this book in 1996 when, as a newly divorced, newly apart mother of four children, my then twelve-year-old daughter asked of a court welfare officer, *'Can I divorce her, too?'* Searching through my doctor, initially, for individuals or organisations who might offer help, advice or consolation through shared experiences, I found nothing and no one.

Crushed and isolated in the long, harrowing days ahead, with physical and emotional energies becoming diluted by fighting a losing battle in the courts as well as with my ex for the right to remain in my children's lives, I became convinced I was 'the only one', the only mother in the world not living with her children and whose children had rejected her.

Since those far off isolated days, through life-changing, life-affirming experiences, but still apart from my children twelve years later, I've finally found that longed-for peace and unexpected happiness deep within myself. But, oh, how I wish I'd had Sarah's book then to give me hope, inspiration and strength when my motherhood was discredited. It would have made my own healing journey so much easier, perhaps even shorter.

If you're newly apart or have been apart for a long time after family breakdown, whether your child or children have been adopted or fostered, whether your child has been abducted abroad or whether your adult child has rejected you after a family row, you'll find tender understanding, practical help and insightful advice from Sarah. Her compassionate tutoring will help ease your sorrow, enabling you to finally reach that place of peaceful harmony within yourself. With Sarah's help, if you want to, you'll acquire the skills and knowledge needed to find that happiness you richly deserve.

In my newly apart days when the internet was still relatively in its infancy, one had to be tenacious in searching for help from professionals, self-help groups or through books. Like Sarah, it was through a happy chance I found MATCH (through Families Need Fathers), eventually discovering other mothers apart, and finding that each one of us had been convinced we'd been 'the only one', each one was eager to pass on anything that might ease our newly apart pain or the anguish of those who'd been apart for one or more decades.

We were astounded to find books had been written about 'us' and that we were not, as we thought, three-headed monsters: Helen Franks's *Mummy Doesn't Live Here Anymore* and Rosie Jackson's *Mothers Who Leave* were passed around and devoured. Since then, with the supersonic growth of the web and unprecedented internet activity, one can more easily access help or advice at a very early stage of being apart. More and more mothers apart, counsellors, therapists, self-help groups, mental health and legal professionals are finding and contacting MATCH fairly easily. However, without exception each new MATCH member is still astonished to find (a) that MATCH exists and (b) that they're *'not the only ones'*. At early MATCH annual general meetings several years ago we used to end our meetings with a cup of tea and a slice of cake, iced with the words, *'Not the only one'*.

Whether newly apart or experienced veterans of several decades, mothers apart have two understandable obsessions: reunion and justice for their children. Such obsessions, if fulfilled, will meet one overriding and overwhelming need: to return to motherhood, which may have been so senselessly and, in some cases, viciously broken. But unfulfilled obsessions, however, after long periods of dwelling on them, have a tendency to make some of us solitary, secretive, hermit-like creatures reluctant to speak about unresolved pain, seemingly unable to find the right place or the right time to do so.

If this sounds like you, or someone you know, and you needing coaxing from your self-imposed bunker, if you're always wondering who or what you should be without your children, or what lies ahead in a supposedly motherless future, you'll find Sarah's practical advice, based, on her long professionalism, invaluable. If you need a friend, a guiding light, trust Sarah to help you to forgive yourself and to take you further than you thought you would go towards that healing place you long to be.

If, despite your sorrows, you've blossomed into a fiercely spirited Boudicca-type warrior with a powerful undiminished outrage, determined to return to mothering your children, you may be relentlessly busy educating and informing yourself on the best means to achieve justice for your children as well as for yourself.

As a battling mother fighting for your own rights, too, to continue to be part of a nurturing, loving family network, no matter where or with whom each family member is living, you may have achieved some success but still may be apart from some or all of your children.

You may have been brought up not to question authority, to trust in 'the law' to deliver justice. You might have offered yourself up for interrogation by legal and court professionals—and, much later, journalists. You may have been submissive, as a newly apart mother, in an attempt to achieve justice for your children's best short-term interests and long-term secure future.

Failure to achieve justice, despite a long, hard committed fight, results in two kinds of brave, courageous mothers apart: those who daily battle melancholy, depression, perhaps debilitating physical or emotional ill-health; and those who fight onwards and upwards towards victory over pain. One member, successful in overturning years of deep hurt, said: 'I reached a very low point after many years of trying to achieve change in my ex and my children when it occurred to me that, if I couldn't change them, I could change myself and my attitudes towards them.'

Perhaps you're still struggling to reach that place. If you're not there yet but want to be, Sarah's practical exercises, deeply rooted in her innate humanitarianism and wisdom, will help you in your own 'journey from despair to peace of mind and happiness' [see her Introduction].

In MATCH there are many stories, told and untold, of courageous battles for justice for children, stories we want to tell widely but have no means to do so. We want to shout from the rooftops, but refrain from doing so that no further damage is inflicted on our children. We keep silent until the press suddenly declare an interest in us, albeit a self-interested, topical one. If we've been refused a fair hearing of our case, either by our children or the courts, there is a compulsive need to speak to the media to get the truth out even if it sometimes turns into an unprepared cascading torrent of self-justification.

Sometimes motherhood has been deliberately destroyed by vindictive family members, sometimes through a court or legal professional's thoughtless negligence or unpreparedness due to heavy caseloads.

However it happens, with the printing of a few hundred words in sometimes trivial publications, the public can make simple judgements on our complex lives, on our fitness to be mothers, before moving on quickly to the next human interest story. As Sarah says in her Introduction, 'There is so much pressure on women to be supermothers, but I believe it's much more healthy and constructive for ourselves and our children when we aim to be good enough, when we aspire to live truthfully, to be who we are instead of trying to live up to someone else's ideal.'

Media interrogations exert a heavy, intensely emotional toll on those who have already undergone lengthy self-interrogation. Stories are retold in our heads so many times as we relive, requestion behaviours or attitudes of everyone involved in our family tragedy to see what could have or might have been done differently to have changed that final, terrible outcome. 'Could have', 'should have', 'would have' frequently occur in MATCH stories.

But when we speak to the media what we're really doing is speaking to our children because we want our children to know, even if we don't see them or hear from them, that we love them unconditionally. We also need them to hear 'our version' of the truth. And we want them to know they weren't 'abandoned' as many have been untruthfully told. But don't think our stories are the defeatist wailings of victims or outcasts. They are clarion calls for justice for our children.

If you've reached the point of needing to talk to journalists so you can 'speak' through them to your children, please read 'Your Story of Healing' in Sarah's consoling **Chapter 2 – Holding up the mirror** in which she says, 'The place to start your healing process is to write a story—the story of how you came to live apart from your child.'

There is no doubt that, even in today's fast-moving, progressive and enlightened world, a mythology still suffocates all mothers, but particularly those not living with their children. Why is a stigma attached to these mothers but not to fathers apart? In the UK those mothers apart who have the status of either a Shared Residence Order or that of Non Resident Parent (custody elsewhere in the western world) bear a heavy burden. As Sarah says in **Chapter 1 – Turning to face the judgement:** *'We live in a world of double standards.'*

Part of MATCH's long-term agenda is to challenge such obsolete, some might say narrow-minded, perspectives of mothers, mothering, and motherhood. Many feel strongly that in the first quarter of the twenty-first century a rigorous debate on the cultural transformation of contemporary parenting in general and contemporary mothering in particular is long overdue.

All responsible, loving, mature parents, after their relationship has come to an end, instinctively want their children to be cherished, safeguarded, respected and nurtured by both parents who care, above all, for their children's long-term best interests. In this the UK government supports them wholeheartedly. On 18 January 2005, the Government published *Parental Separation: Children's Needs and Parents' Responsibilities, Next*

Steps. This document responded to the consultation on the Green Paper on the same topic which was launched on 21 July 2004: *'Parental separation affects many children and their families. Some three million of the twelve million children in this country have experienced the separation of their parents.'* (Ministerial Foreword, 2004 Green Paper) Both parents should be actively encouraging and respecting children's contact with all loving family members, embodying the government's view that *'After separation, both parents should have responsibility for, and a meaningful relationship with, their children, so long as it is safe. This is the view of most people in our society. And it is the current legal position.'*

Should it really matter then to our contemporary, fast-changing society which parent children live with? Why should it be necessary to pass judgement on that parent living apart from their children? The ultimate objective of what I would term 'powerful, passionate equal parenting' is to ensure that children are loved by both parents in equal measure even if contact time is, for commonsense reasons, unequal. A child's parents are for life, not just for the duration of his parents' relationship.

Children's best interests should be the overarching cornerstone of government policy, as well respected research has shown overwhelmingly the power of a loving family network to transform, sustain and enrich all our lives forever.

Until such time as society reshapes highly judgemental views on mothers living apart from their children, such mothers will need help to come to terms with their pain and sorrow. Sarah Hart has set a gold standard in offering therapeutic support for such mothers and, on behalf of all past, present and future MATCH members, I would like to express our gratitude for her passionate commitment to helping us, our admiration for the courageous honesty she has shown in acknowledging her own story, and in sharing her compassionate wisdom so we can begin to reconstruct our lives and start to be happy. None of us deserves less than this.

Penny Cross

Chair, Mothers Apart from Their Children (MATCH)
and author of *Lost Children: A Guide for Separating Parents* (Velvet Glove, 2000)

About Sarah Hart

Twenty years ago—three months after leaving my husband, taking our two small children with me and returning to my country of birth—I took my eldest child back half way around the world, to live with him in our family home.

Like many mothers apart the circumstances of my separation were far from simple. I married as a teenager and nine years later, when it became intolerable for me to remain with my husband, I found myself facing extremely limited options, living in a country in a state of political unrest, with little in the way of a social security system and without any extended family on the same continent, let alone country.

I never for one moment imagined that I'd leave either of my children with my ex but over a period of a few short weeks of emotional turmoil, no economic means, unconstructive advice and a lack of knowledge about organisations I now know would have been able to help me, the unimaginable happened.

In the years that followed, I learned that life as a mother apart is a dichotomy between the real reason, the true story of why many women leave or find themselves separated from their child, and the stereotype of women who are seen to have abandoned their children. Even today, when amicable separations occur (in as much as divorce and separation can be amicable), mothers who don't live with their children are regarded as at best an oddity and at worst, unnatural and selfish.

It's this tension between the real reason, the whole picture of how it came to be that a woman lives apart from her child and the combination of other people's judgements and how women judge themselves, which leads to a split. And it's this divide that causes confusion, creates secrets, induces guilt—that cuts mothers apart off from their truth and inner knowing about the reality of their situation when they left, that saps their self-esteem, knocks their confidence, makes them mistrust their instincts and forget their motivations.

During the first year of my separation from my child—quite by chance, which of course is really absolute synchronicity—I came across a self-help organisation called MATCH (now a charity), established for mothers who live apart from their children. I discovered that there are many reasons why women don't live permanently with their children. In those early days, it was through MATCH members that I learned that I wasn't alone and we supported each other by sharing our experiences—hard and heartbreaking times, as well as our successes, joys and wisdom.

Wanting to heal my pain and gain a better understanding of what had happened in my life, I went into therapy which, after a few years, created a desire in me to learn more in order to help others. Fourteen years ago I qualified as a counsellor and since then have worked with women dealing with a spectrum of issues including: loss, separation, living apart from children, painful childhood histories, relationships, co-dependency and work–life issues. Becoming aware of the growing burden on women to manage successful home and work lives simultaneously, I studied the subject further by completing a master's degree in social policy. It's this pressure of having to be it all, to do it all and have it all from those around us—including the media and those who govern us, who dictate the norm—together with the Superwoman expectations we have of ourselves that I help women to unravel, whether I'm working in my role as women's professional and personal group facilitator or one to one.

Over the years I have worked hard and long to understand and learn to live with what in my case was deep loss, pain, guilt and shame at living apart from my child. As time passed I began to realise that working hard at developing and healing myself was in fact the exact opposite of what I needed to do. There is so much pressure on women to be Supermothers, but I believe it's much more healthy and constructive for ourselves and our children when we aim to be good enough, when we aspire to live truthfully, to be who we are instead of trying to live up to someone else's ideal.

It is possible to live and love this way and this is what I aim to share with you. It takes insight, tenacity, the company of others who understand and some guidance along the way … and it's my heartfelt hope that this book will provide you with some of the knowledge, encouragement and inspiration for *your* journey.

Sarah Hart

March 2008

If you'd like to find out more or obtain details about counselling, please visit my website www.sarahhart.co.uk

Introduction

Take heart, mother apart: the journey from despair to peace of mind and happiness

'Why did you leave them?'
'How could you have allowed it to happen?'
'How do you live with it?'

If you are a mother living apart from your child, I'm certain you will have been asked these questions and other variations. The enquirer is at best surprised and at worst incredulous and shocked when we talk about our circumstances. Sometimes they fall silent, and dealing with their embarrassed confusion and hasty attempts to change the subject can be as difficult as those people who are eager to know more. Questions are thrown quick and fast, and as we try to find the words to explain, we feel judgement soaking into us like dye—the tarnishing proof that we are unnatural mothers. A mother who abandons. The woman who has committed the ultimate taboo.

As a mother apart, I know how you feel. As a counsellor, I understand that the experiences of women in your position can be complicated, and your feelings bewildering and sometimes extreme.

'If anyone had told me that by the time he was six we'd be separated I'd never have believed them—we were incredibly close.'

Danielle

'Seeing other mothers enjoying their children is still so upsetting. How did this happen to me? Will we ever have good times together again?'

Jayne

Regret, guilt, high anxiety and depression—many mothers apart feel like they have received a life sentence of pain. Take heart: this book will support you. It will help you make positive changes and find acceptance for what you cannot change.

Who this book is for

A Mother Apart is written for women who have chosen to live apart from their child as well as those who are suffering separation that had nothing to do with a direct, personal decision to leave a child, including:

Mothers with **regular** contact with their children:

- Non-resident mothers. In other words, women who are divorced or separated and are not regarded as the primary carer of her child by the courts.

- Mothers who have shared residency. Part-time Mums who consider themselves to be co-parents with the child's father.

- Mothers whose children live with a carer other than their father.

Mothers with **irregular** contact:

- Mothers whose circumstances might be any of the above but for whatever reason, their relationship with their child or the child's primary carer has become strained and contact has become irregular.

- Long distance mothers. Living far away from a child, perhaps in another country, makes regular contact difficult.

Mothers who have **no contact** with their children:

- Circumstances can vary greatly, with some mothers having been granted shared residency and contact by the courts but who still suffer from parental alienation.

Various chapters of *A Mother Apart* can also support women who have had their children abducted by partners living in another country, mothers whose children are in foster care, women whose children have been adopted, mothers in prison and the like.

While all chapters might not be immediately relevant to all mothers apart, the book will provide guidance and help as personal circumstances change.

Partners, family and friends

The strong feelings and often complex circumstances of mothers living apart from their children is, at times, baffling and difficult for loved ones. The aim of the book is also to help de-mystify the status of being a mother apart and provide insights and solutions to partners, relatives and friends—or anyone wanting to support a woman living apart from a child.

Perhaps you'll recognise your circumstances in some examples of how a woman becomes or experiences being a mother apart below:

- A shared residency order that doesn't work well in practice. A mother may find the reality of being a part-time parent very difficult or painful: The child's father could be obstructive and not encourage a good, ongoing relationship between a mother and child. Or a child might blame a mother for the separation and a once loving relationship changes. Or a teenage child becomes less interested in seeing their mother as they gain independence.

- A mother was the main breadwinner in the family and, by choice or default, the father was regarded as the primary carer by the courts.

- A mother who leaves her children in the family home with their father as she doesn't want to disrupt their everyday lives.

- A mother who leaves the family home for a short period of time because she needs space to make a decision about her marriage and finds that relationships have deteriorated and decisions have been made about residency in her absence.

- A mother goes into hospital suffering from depression to find that home life doesn't return to how it was before she became unwell. Her child might be living with another carer or her relationship with her partner has broken down.

- A mother who loses residency because of drug or alcohol addiction.

- Some mothers even have a shared residency order but have no contact due to parental alienation.

These scenarios highlight just a few of the many variations of what it means to be a mother apart. Very often, the die is cast rapidly and so I'll add:

- *Any situation* where decisions are made quickly, in times of high stress and few emotional or financial resources together with a good pinch of guilt, can lead to a life as a mother apart and outcomes that cause pain and regret.

Why this book was written

As many mothers apart will testify, it can be difficult to find understanding and support for our circumstances as women living apart from our children.

> *'I want to learn what I need to do to feel better about being separated from my daughter. I want to know how to manage being in a new relationship and to help my partner understand what I'm going through. He tries but he doesn't really understand.'*
>
> *Olivia*

> *'How do I cope with my feelings as I live as resident mother to one child and long distance mother to two others? More than anything, I want to know that I'm not the bad, mad, crazy woman I sometimes feel myself to be.'*
>
> *Natalie*

> *'My ex-partner and his new wife make things as difficult as they can for me. It breaks my heart to think that they have so much influence in Sammy's life.'*
>
> *Alex*

> *'I need information on what to expect and how to handle mothering apart as my children grow up. Because I don't see them regularly I visualise them being younger than they actually are. I always seem to be about five years behind.'*
>
> *Helen*

The purpose of *A Mother Apart* is to help *you*. Your well-being is its primary focus. I urge you put on hold anything you've learnt or heard that concerns itself with how much children suffer without a full-time mother. The combination of what others think of our actions and how we judge ourselves can distort our self-knowledge and personal awareness. In our confusion it's easy to blur what we imagine our children feel with our own emotions. The book's contents will help you separate your feelings from those of your child, media views on parenthood and the opinions of child psychologists.

This book is different because it's not going to tell you that you should have put the needs of your child before your own.

Perhaps the reason you're separated from your child is because you *did* put your feelings and desires before your child's.

> *'I needed to get out. I don't regret leaving, I think it was the right thing to do for all our sakes, but I'm still made to feel guilty.'*
>
> *Vickie*

Maybe the reason you left was because you truly needed to get away for the sake of your emotional health.

> *'I only planned to leave for a month to have a rest and sort things out in my mind. I couldn't believe how much had changed in just four weeks—my husband's hostility, the children turned against me, even the locks had been changed.'*
>
> *Jayne*

Whatever your reason for leaving, the emphasis of this book is on you, and the effects of the separation on your well-being, self-esteem, your choices, your future. Why? Because if you focus on *your* needs and feelings, become more aware of *what* happened, *why* it happened and its deeper meaning, and learn how to treat yourself with compassion, the change in you will be the best thing for your child.

I HAVE NEVER COME ACROSS A WOMAN WHO JUST UP AND LEFT ONE DAY ON A FLIGHT OF FANCY—EVEN THOUGH IT MIGHT HAVE LOOKED LIKE IT TO THE OUTSIDE WORLD.

So saying, my role on these pages is to help you truly accept your life as a mother apart from her child, to come to terms with your feelings, and challenge any negative beliefs and behaviour that cause you pain. My aim is to show you that you can change how you think about yourself as a mother apart in a way that doesn't deny what you feel. Chances are you aren't aware of what a great mother you really are. Your capacity to hold on to your status of being a mother living apart from your child, your ability to hold the space of mother inside you even though you might not have current contact with your child, is quite remarkable. The fact that you've picked up this book shows both your commitment to yourself and the strength you have to keep trying, to hang in there, to hold on to loving deeply from afar. I applaud you. However you came to be separated from your child, whatever action or inaction you took, it was not something you did lightly; internal pressures, childhood legacies, oppressive marriages, a lack of self-belief, self-awareness, emotional support and economic means lead to desperate situations and limited options.

This book will show you how to live a full and happy life despite living apart from your child.

Does this sound impossible to you? Maybe you are locked in bitter battles over residency or contact, or are newly separated from your child. My heart goes out to you.

You are not alone.

Twenty years ago, I left my daughter with her father. I imagined I was the only woman in the world who had done such a thing.

There are millions of women around the world who live separately from their children. Your status is more common than perhaps you realise. Living arrangements following divorce and separation vary enormously. However, because of the reactions and responses they receive, many mothers choose not to tell anyone if they have a child that lives elsewhere. Sometimes, women say nothing because their circumstances are just too painful to talk about. Keeping quiet about the fact that we have children means we can spare ourselves from opening up the wound. But denying our children to the world (and sometimes to ourselves), doesn't serve us. Before long we find we're living a secret life, an existence split in two by our attempts to protect ourselves, which leaves us feeling increasingly disconnected, deceitful and worn down by having to maintain our public pretence.

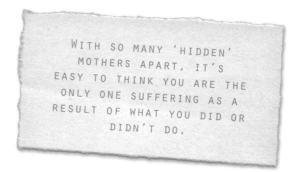

WITH SO MANY 'HIDDEN' MOTHERS APART, IT'S EASY TO THINK YOU ARE THE ONLY ONE SUFFERING AS A RESULT OF WHAT YOU DID OR DIDN'T DO.

'I have a double life: a mother on access weekends and at holidays and during 9 to 5, a professional woman. Nobody at work knows I have children.'

Imogen

It doesn't have to be like this. You can come to terms with decisions you have made, your circumstances as a mother and live truthfully and harmoniously. There is another way.

**However far apart, whatever the nature of your separation,
you can find serenity and restore lost dignity.**

Will this book help you?

To assess whether *A Mother Apart* can help you, answer the questions below as honestly as you can. Answer *true* even if the question is somewhat true for you and *false* if it's not very true or not at all true.

1. I feel guilty about living apart from my child

2. I feel a sense of shame when I talk or think about having left my child

3. I have feelings of loss and grief about being separated from my child

4. I regret some of the decisions I made which resulted in my child living apart from me

5. I sometimes despair of ever having a good relationship with my child

6. I don't feel that I'm a good mother

7. I tend to be secretive about the fact that I live apart from my child

8. I feel judged by other people

9. I find it hard to talk about my personal circumstances

10. I have a difficult relationship with the father of the child I live apart from

11. I don't feel it would work for either of us if my child lived permanently with me

12. I find it hard to communicate with my child

13. My confidence and self-esteem are low

14. I feel rejected by my child

15. It's painful to think that a stepmother is, or perhaps will be, 'replacing' me

16. I feel like I give too much emotionally or materially to my child when we spend time together

17. I feel it's all my fault when I see my child struggling with life

18. If I'm honest, I sometimes feel relieved that my child doesn't live with me

19. I want a new relationship with a partner but the difficulties of living apart from my child get in the way

20. Guilt makes me feel like I don't have the right to be happy

If you've answered true to four or more questions, you're likely to be struggling with your circumstances as a mother living apart from your child. The feelings of mothers apart can be complex and contradictory, so even if you've answered true to one or two questions, you are likely to find this book comforting and informative.

How you will benefit

I want to take you gently to the heart of what it means to live separately from your child. I want to confront the taboo and show you how to enrich your life from a very unique position. You will find practical solutions to help you find the best way of dealing with important milestones, as well as little difficulties along the way. Throughout the book, you will find a variety of activities designed to explore how you feel and which will help you to choose more positive and resourceful ways of thinking and living. These processes of personal discovery have the potential to be an illuminating and powerful impetus for change.

As you work through this book, you will find help and support to:

- Accept that you did the best you could at the time, under difficult circumstances

- Free yourself from guilt and shame

- Grieve your loss and move on with an open heart

- Learn the art of big-hearted mothering: deep love from afar, over time

- Acknowledge and take responsibility for your actions and learn when not to take responsibility

- Live your life a day at a time, despite feeling intense sorrow and grief some days

- Let go of trying to control anyone but yourself

- Learn to love and enjoy your child in the moment, without fearing for tomorrow

- Find and maintain your dignity, and be proud of your status of mother

- Try again when you forget or struggle to manage any of the above

There are a number of ways to use this book and I invite you to read, write and take action.

A Mother Apart will support you to look courageously at all aspects of mothering apart. It is likely that as you read and complete the exercises you will feel comforted and re-assured, as well as challenged and sad at times. This is perfectly normal.

I urge you to be as honest and as gentle with yourself as possible, in equal measure. If you find an exercise particularly challenging, have a break to allow new insights to filter through. Give yourself time to reflect as well as doing something completely different. Physical exercise, being out in nature or doing any activity that relaxes you is ideal for balancing a process of change and growth within yourself. For times when you feel particularly vulnerable, a warm, soothing bath, soft music and candles can be a comforting antidote.

And finally ...

It is my dearest wish that through the tools, methods and practical strategies that I offer in this book, you will feel less alone, gain a greater insight into why you feel the way you do and will feel encouraged to make changes that will allow you to feel happy, confident and at peace with yourself and others in your life. You *so* deserve it!

Chapter 1

Turning to face the judgement

Before we can set about freeing ourselves from painful feelings and negative beliefs, it's important that we know where they originate from and exactly what they are.

> *"Is Ben your only child?" I always wait for that question. It's a natural enough thing for other people to ask but I dread it. My face goes red and my stomach knots. When I talk about my son from my first marriage living away from me, words just tumble out. I feel I have to explain my actions, explain my life. Sometimes when I just can't face justifying any of it, I lie to avoid the reaction. Generally it all pops out or it stays firmly locked inside me, though it's true to say that there are also certain people I just know not to say a single word to. I just can't bear to think that I'm being judged.'*
>
> *Fern*

Perhaps you recognise these two ways of handling a question about being a mother—the outpouring or denial?

As a mother apart, you'll probably know that talking about your circumstances, your life and how it is that you are separated from your child can leave you feeling exposed, guilty, grieving, angry and other difficult emotions. You might notice that how you feel sometimes seems to be determined by the reaction of the person you're talking to. At other times, your listener is moved by what you say and is understanding and kind, but somehow you're still left feeling lots of similar feelings which can be confusing. What's going on?

Mothers apart experience a double whammy.
We face the judgement of the outside world, usually the actual responses
from the people we come into contact with and what we read and hear in the
media, and we are also judged by our 'inside' world.

This means we are often very good at being our own worst enemy, capable of criticising and condemning ourselves for decisions that we did or didn't make. You'll most likely have had the experience of judgement from the outside world triggering you to turn on yourself, blaming yourself for past actions or inaction. During darker moments, you may well experience your inner judge or critic doing its best to hurt you, all by itself, unprovoked by anyone or anything. Let's throw a bit more light on this debilitating pair—the outer and inner judgements.

Outer judgement

Stereotyped motherhood

We live in a world of gender double standards. Even though there is growing political support for men to play a more active role in their children's upbringing through paternity leave and the business world's gradual support for flexible, family friendly working, women are still regarded as the primary caregivers. Despite the rising numbers of lone parent men, it's still more socially acceptable for a single mother to care for her children than a lone father. Even the 2007 edition of Roget's *New Millennium Thesaurus* defines the verb *mother* as 'care for' and *father* 'create'. Synonyms listed reflect clear differences in our cultural understanding and expectations of both states. To *father*—beget, breed, engender, establish, invent, make, originate, parent, procreate, sire, spawn. To *mother*—bring forth, cherish, fuss over, indulge, minister to, nurse, nurture, pamper, protect, raise, rear, serve, spoil, tend, wait on. Mothering is a tall order!

Now while this book is an emotional and practical guide it's important to consider the impact of culture, mythology and politics, as they fuel what we experience as external judgements from the world.

There's a gap between political support of parenthood, and the views and attitudes within our society. Increasing levels of parental leave and the right to negotiate flexible working means that more women are becoming joint breadwinners. Indeed, the heavy burden of being a joint breadwinner and primary care giver within a floundering relationship is one of the reasons why mothers leave the family home. There are also increasing numbers of househusbands, which results in men being given residency of children on the basis that they are primary care givers.

These changes to traditional roles are a contributory factor to some mothers leaving. From research currently available, we know that the numbers of women living apart from their children is growing. But even though greater numbers are leaving, it is still seen as more natural for a man to look for personal and professional fulfilment outside the home than a woman.

**When fathers leave children it is considered a sad but fairly
normal occurrence. By and large, fathering is regarded more in terms of
creating a child than nurturing it.**

Some women make the very difficult decision of choosing part-time motherhood instead of being a full-time resentful Mum. In her book *Unbecoming Mothers: The Social Production of Maternal Absence*, Diana L. Gustafson, writing about how motherhood is stereotyped and concludes that, 'A woman who is unwilling or unable to perform her motherly duties is thought to be motivated by selfishness, self-absorption, and self-indulgence—all individual defects. Given these ways of thinking and talking about mothering, a woman who lives apart from her birth children would seem to be the epitome of the bad mother—an unnatural, aberrant woman.'

In my experience, these descriptors of mothers apart—'selfishness', 'self-absorption' and 'self-indulgence' are a far cry from the real reasons many women are separated from their children. Indeed, perhaps the most frequent reason a mother leaves her child with their father is to ensure their stability in the family home and their home town, at the expense of her own feelings and maternal longing.

My work with women in personal and professional development groups, even with women leaders, has an important focus in encouraging women to think twice about putting others first, to hold back on the impulse to give too much on the nurture front. Many of us can quickly lose focus of our priorities, career development, goals and dreams when we pick up on signals which urge us to take care of others. Women still find it difficult to work out whether 'giving too much' is a natural instinct or an 'I should' behaviour, in other words, a need within them to be seen as nurturing and caring.

IT IS TABOO FOR WOMEN TO LEAVE THEIR CHILDREN. IF YOU HAVE FELT JUDGED BY OTHERS, IT'S HARDLY SURPRISING. THOSE WHO HAVE NOT HAD TO FACE OUR OPTIONS, OFTEN AT TIMES OF ACUTE STRESS, COULD EASILY SUBSCRIBE TO THE CULTURAL STEREOTYPE OF THE MOTHER WHO WOULD FIGHT TO THE DEATH RATHER THAN LIVE WITHOUT HER CHILDREN.

Let's take another look at that definition of what a mother is supposed to do: bring forth, cherish, fuss over, indulge, minister to, nurse, nurture, pamper, protect, raise, rear, serve, spoil, tend, wait on. I don't know about you, but it's easy for me to feel overwhelmed by that list. For mothers living apart from children, women still being defined as principally living through their relationships with others, coupled with the high ideals of the role of motherhood, creates strong judgement from the outside world. The ideology of selfless motherhood results in mothers apart usually being regarded as unnatural, odd or strange and by some; and heartless, selfish or cruel by others.

JUDGEMENT FROM THE OUTSIDE WORLD IS FUELLED BY STORIES OF ABANDONING MOTHERS, BOTH REAL AND FICTIONAL, SUCH AS HENRIK IBSEN'S PLAY, *A DOLL'S HOUSE* AND THE FILM, *KRAMER VS. KRAMER*. PERHAPS THE MOST HIGHLY PROFILED, REAL LIFE EXAMPLE OF OUR TIME IS FRANCES SHAND KYDD LEAVING HER FIVE-YEAR-OLD DAUGHTER, DIANA SPENCER, WHO WAS DEEMED PERMANENTLY SCARRED AND VULNERABLE AS A RESULT. ROSIE JACKSON IN *MOTHERS WHO LEAVE*, POINTS OUT THE LITTLE ACKNOWLEDGED FACT THAT DIANA'S MOTHER FOUGHT HARD TO GAIN CUSTODY AFTER LEAVING A DIFFICULT MARRIAGE. ON LOSING CUSTODY FRANCES MANAGED TO MAINTAIN SUPPORTIVE RELATIONSHIPS WITH HER CHILDREN DESPITE CONSIDERABLE OPPOSITION.

Flying in the face of the stereotypical views of the self-centred, abandoning mother, a recent study of the relative frequencies of non-resident parents' involvement with their children shows that absent mothers are *more* involved in their children's lives than absent fathers. Absent mothers have *more* extended visitations and higher levels of telephone and letter contact than absent fathers. I am deeply moved and in awe of the lengths to which some mothers apart have gone: phoning a child on a regular basis despite a hostile response from an ex-partner, sending letters and cards every week just to maintain contact, having meetings with teachers to get regular updates on their child, raising money for travel costs and so on. Although painful, many mothers keep attempting contact even when a relationship with their child seems like an impossibility. Indeed, many mothers apart make up some of the selfless few of the world.

The universal mother dump

Our society, which views motherhood as the most sacred bond, is made up of individuals with their own perceptions and attitudes towards mothers who leave. This is an unpredictable component for you as you live your life apart from your child. You can gain knowledge of the politics, observe the culture and trace the mythology. What you cannot foresee or control are the opinions of others towards your circumstances.

Other people's attitudes towards you will be defined by their own experiences of motherhood.

For many people, 'mother' evokes powerful reactions. Their relationship with their mother, the all-powerful caregiver to them as babies, young children, adolescents and adults will shape their response to you. How much they loved, respected, hated, admired and needed their mothers—how much they felt loved, accepted, supported, valued, put down, rejected and yes, whether or not they felt neglected or abandoned— will all come your way.

In responding to you, other people might acknowledge a difficult relationship with their mother, a lack of acceptance, unmet needs or perhaps telling a story of their own separation. On the other hand, your listener might not be consciously aware of any link between your circumstances and their past. As you tell your story, it could hook into their unconscious hurt, anger and unmet needs, resulting in their judgement and criticism of your actions.

Judgements by others

I explained to Tim I would miss him but this was something I had to do, and I would be back for Christmas.
Let her who has never fallen throw the first stony judgement.

In the Dark and Still Moving—Anne Geraghty

It's no mistake that Anne Geraghty uses *her* not *he*, pronouncing, 'Let *her* who has never fallen throw the first stony judgement', when she writes about how she told her son Tim that she was leaving him with his father for a while, in order to follow her spiritual quest to India.

You might be surprised to find strong judgement of your actions by other women, particularly other mothers.

In my experience there are three types of mother in particular who react strongly. I mention these three without judgement, as what they experience as mothers is intense in different ways. The first is the mother whose child has died. Mother apart, Elaine, explains below.

'I received a lot of hostility from a woman I used to chat with at the school gate. After I moved out of the family home, I bumped into her one day. I was shocked by her critical tone. She didn't exactly say she thought I was wrong to leave my daughter at home but I felt disapproved of. I felt really hurt. A few years later I heard her daughter had become

sick with a terminal illness. Although I didn't see a lot of her, I always sensed her resentment towards me when we met in passing.'

Although this was a painful experience for Elaine, she understood the other woman's hostility towards her. She explained, 'It's not that I think it is fair or that I deserve it. I understand that to her I have a daughter and, through choice, live without her. Having lost her daughter in such a tragic way, I can see that the pain and troubles I have faced in my life probably seem self-induced and beyond her understanding.' This type of reaction is very difficult to deal with and Elaine shows remarkable sensitivity and courage in understanding the other mother's view on the world instead of allowing her judgement and resentment to batter her self-esteem.

In a similar vein, it is understandable for women who have had a miscarriage or who are struggling to become pregnant to respond in ways that are linked to their own loss, frustration and grief rather than with understanding of our situation. Finally, it's wise to be mindful of the strong maternal feelings and bond of new mothers. Perhaps, like me, you can remember the intense protective feelings in the early weeks of motherhood when the thought of being separated from your child would lead to nightmares and fantasies of fighting off anyone who came between you and your baby.

Of course, judgement can come from men too. You might experience it from others you know well and people who hardly know you. Either way it can come as an unpleasant surprise. An elderly male neighbour that you used to look in on will no longer talk to you. The chap who owns the corner shop isn't as friendly as he used to be. The child minder who used to confide in you keeps it 'strictly business' when you pick up your child on Friday afternoons.

> LET'S BE CLEAR—ANOTHER PERSON'S JUDGEMENT OF YOU IS NOT 'THE TRUTH'.

Please remember that when you are stung by a response it will often have little to do with you and your actions—and more to do with the reactions of others, shaped by their own experience, culture and personal history.

Inner judgement

Inner judgement is linked to the thoughts and feelings you have about yourself as a mother living apart from your child. Whether and how you judge yourself shapes the internal messages you give yourself, and ultimately, how you feel about yourself.

If you judge yourself harshly for being apart from your child, the critical voice inside you is likely to give you messages that say things like you're selfish, cruel, uncaring, beyond forgiveness—whatever it knows will hook in deep and do the damage. As if it wasn't bad enough to endure judgement from the outside world, our inner critic is capable of delivering some debilitating blows. After all, no one else knows our weaknesses as well as we do.

Negative inner judgement erodes self-esteem and destroys confidence.

What is the difference between these two? Your self-esteem is the overall opinion you have of yourself. It is the value you attach to yourself and is affected by how you view and judge yourself. The essence of self-esteem is your central belief about yourself and it cannot be faked or put on—unlike confidence. Perhaps you've had the experience of feeling really nervous but pretending you weren't, acting as if you were confident and finding that you came across to others that way. If you take action and do something you're anxious about, instead of telling yourself you can't, you can raise your confidence, which in turn increases your self-esteem, your honest opinion of yourself.

It's important to recognise that living with critical inner judgements, whether they be conscious or not, causes you damage.

Guilt and shame are two inner judgements that are particularly difficult and almost inherent to mothers apart. In order to stop their debilitating effects, we need to first to examine them to understand them a bit more.

Guilt

'They sometimes ask "Why did you leave us?"—especially my middle son, who isn't as close to his father as the others. I feel so bad. I try and explain but I never know how much to say about how difficult it was between their father and me. I don't want to burden them or cause more upset. I feel really awful about it—guilty, guilty, guilty.'

Helen

Guilt is often muddled with shame. Making the distinction between the two is useful for finding ways to relieve ourselves from their control. Guilt is the painful feeling that comes when we do something that transgresses a personal value or standard that we've set ourselves—when we've broken our word or a commitment to someone else, when our behaviour has hurt somebody or when we've committed a crime or broken the law. It is a feeling that is triggered by our actions and it can be connected to something that we've done in the past or in the present. Healthy guilt, on the other hand, lets us know our conscious is operating. It acts as our internal barometer. It can guide us to face up to reality, find solutions to problems, make amends, right a wrong or put effort into a relationship that is important to us.

But we can also feel guilty about something that we imagine we've done. Feelings of guilt then become unhealthy and unhelpful to us. They can immobilise us. They also cause us to overreact. We take all the blame instead of half of it. Guilt gets in the way of our ability to live freely and it takes away our peace of mind.

> *'Even after living apart from Jodie for ten years, I still feel guilty. Now that she's nearly twenty, I feel even more worn down when she comes to stay. I let her get away with too much when she was younger. I didn't want to upset her so I gave in when I should have said "No". I didn't want to be the disciplinarian; I wanted our time together to go smoothly. But mostly I felt too guilty to—I imagined that she'd say, "You left me, you don't have the right."'*
>
> *Yvette*

Most mothers apart from their children struggle with feelings of guilt to a lesser or greater degree. The combined forces of outer judgement from the world and inner judgement leaves some women with twinges of guilt and others frozen rigid by it.

> *'It's so frustrating. Even though my ex and I agreed that it was best for all of us, especially our children, that he would stay in our house with the children as he worked from home. Even though our parting was amicable and three years have passed and the children seem settled, I still feel really guilty.'*
>
> *Vickie*

It's vital to face guilt head on. The price of not acknowledging, not having a closer look, not sifting through what is healthy and unhealthy guilt and working it though, is high. Not to do so keeps you vulnerable to the body blows of other people's judgement and the hard time you are capable of giving yourself. Feeling regret for action and inaction needs to be looked at. Thinking that you have or are hurting, damaging or ruining other people's lives must be faced up to. Believing that you are responsible for other people's misery, that you have caused them to suffer, that it is or was your fault, all need to be held up in the cold light of day and examined closely.

Guilt can make you over-responsible—make you give too much and expect too little, cause you to lose touch with your intuition, make you oversensitive, block and mask other feelings and deceive you into believing things that just aren't true.

But feelings of guilt can also be your liberator—pointing the way out, the power source of change. Investigated and reviewed they can act as your barometer to gauge what you need to put right and change before letting go of this malicious saboteur.

Shame

> *'I can remember feeling so burdened by shame that I couldn't play with my son; living apart from my daughter I didn't feel worthy of having another child to love, play and have fun with. A voice inside would tell me I was a sham.'*
>
> *Lucy*

Whereas guilt makes us feel bad from *doing* wrong, we feel shame from believing that we *are* wrong, that we haven't lived up to our personal expectations or the expectations of others. Shame is that belittling feeling that we experience when we believe that part of us is bad. Guilt can be seen as something that can be put right or fixed but shame can feel like it will always be there. Shame can make us feel like there is no help for us, no chance of anything changing as the feeling of there being something very wrong with us is buried deep inside us. We feel embarrassed and stigmatised about living apart from our children.

> *'It's always there, something to be ashamed of. I agreed that he could have custody and handed over the day-to-day care of my two children. I can still see the look of judgement on the faces of his family, especially his mother. The truth is I had to leave for my own sanity; I couldn't live a lie any longer. Becoming a mother before I was ready has a lot to do with me feeling as suffocated as I did. Some days I know I made the right decision but other times I'm weighed down with the secret shame I have inside.'*
>
> *Natalie*

Around shame there is a sense of needing to hide. Shame separates us from other people because it feels incommunicable and so we have the urge to hide parts of ourselves, keep them secret. In *Women Who Run With the Wolves*, Clarissa Pinkola Estés writes about the keeping of secrets associated with shame. Estés says that women's secrets are usually connected to having violated a social or moral code of their culture rather than 'having told a bald face lie or having done a purposeful meanness that caused someone else trouble or pain'. Furthermore women's secrets, particularly those related to freedom, are usually seen by their culture as being shamefully wrong for women but not for men.

Secrets we keep and how we suffer

So what are the secrets of women apart from their children? For each of us it will be different as we all have our own shame hot spots linked to our personal history, culture and values. Typically they include 'shoulds' or 'coulds' as this is the language of judgement: I should have done more of or less of ...; I could have tried harder or stuck at it longer; If only I had been quicker or slower, done it sooner or later, been more astute or less picky, more accepting, less demanding; I should have been less passive or less aggressive; I could have given more or taken less—and on and on our judgement goes, weaving a shroud into which we hide our secret.

And then comes our crunch line: we left our child, we took them back, they were taken from us, depending on our circumstances. We tend to view this in a condemnatory way that fails to consider the whole picture—to include truths like having no or low levels of support, a lack of finances, emotional breakdown, physical breakdown, being a victim of a partner's emotional or physical abuse, our children's views on where they wanted to live, our deep knowing that if we didn't leave we would have gone under or that we just understood that we could not continue being a mother in that way, under that roof.

Not to face shame after a trauma as great as leaving a child cuts us off from far more than we realise. It's like sustaining a back injury and not relating the pain in your neck, legs and arms as being your body's way of trying to compensate for the real problem area. Sometimes you don't realise how extensive an injury is, how much strain there has been on other parts of the body, until the site of the initial damage is healed.

Any shame we suffer gets in the way of being able to grieve our losses and move on. It cuts us off from receiving love from a partner or friends. It could prevent us from showing love towards and relating in a healthy way to any other children we might have. Not confronting shame could choke creativity, fun and spontaneity, stopping us from receiving compliments and eroding self-esteem.

IT DOESN'T HAVE TO BE LIKE THIS. REMEMBER YOU HAVE THE RIGHT TO FEEL GOOD ABOUT YOURSELF. NO MATTER HOW LONG YOU'VE LIVED SEPARATELY FROM YOUR CHILD, IT'S POSSIBLE TO LET GO OF ANY SHAME AND UNNECESSARY GUILT YOU MIGHT FEEL.

Wanting to be forgiven

'I know I have hurt my children and I pay the price. My son is loving towards me and pleased to see me but my daughter won't or can't forgive me. I don't blame her—how can I when I can't forgive myself.'

Imogen

Some mothers apart want to be forgiven by their children, themselves, their families and the world. They long to hear 'I forgive you' in the hope that the words will take away the painful feelings they live with. But to want forgiveness is to believe that you have committed an act for which you need to be pardoned.

Perhaps there are things you have done for which you will decide you'd like to make amends. But to focus your attention on being forgiven means that you could be looking outside of yourself for approval for a long time—indeed it might never come. A much more empowering way is to concentrate on understanding yourself and your motives better and treating yourself with the gentleness you deserve.

The primary aim of the process we will soon embark upon is to truly accept ourselves and the decisions we made. Learning the art of acceptance, for our actions and their consequences, means that we are on the road to personal freedom and self-respect. Our goal is to accept that we did the best we could at that time with the resources available to us, irrespective of what others might think. Stop a moment to take that in … *You did the best you could at the time, being who you were then, others being as they were, in your home, cultural and economic environment.*

A voice in your head might be telling you otherwise right now, but don't let that put you off. In fact, hearing what that voice has to say has an important role in your journey towards acceptance, so make a note of it—we'll come back to it in the next chapter.

The process of acceptance begins by:

- Exploring the stereotypical views of motherhood

- Being aware of the opinions of individual people in your life

- Listening to and reality checking the judgement you hold deep within yourself

And the way for us to do this is to reflect on how we came to be separated from our child or why we left. The whole story. Even the details we might try to hide. All of it. Openly and truthfully. We need to lay our story out and go through it carefully, as the only way out is through.

This is your chance to hold what you've perhaps been dreading up to the light. To come face to face with it, examine what it is made of in order to free yourself from any unhealthy guilt, shame and desire to be forgiven and begin to see where these feelings come from. To see where you've come from. And then decide what is relevant, true and important to keep—as well as what is outdated or inappropriate. In essence, you're going to do a de-junk.

If we want to build healthy relationships with our children, we need first to have a healthy relationship with ourselves. This means treating ourselves with the understanding and compassion we deserve. Only in this way can we build our self-esteem. And this is the work of the next chapter.

Chapter 2

Holding up the mirror

Now that we have a better understanding of the impact of stereotyped motherhood on mothers apart, how the judgement from the world effects us and what our internal judgements are made of, it's time to shift the emphasis from the collective and hold up the mirror to explore your own, personal circumstances.

In this chapter you will be guided through a liberating, three stage exercise called 'Your Story of Healing', to de-junk your outer and inner judgements—the judgements that affect *you* specifically. This process will, with care and sensitivity, help you to revisit the circumstances of your separation from your child and provide a replacement strategy to help you substitute any harsh judgements, out of date beliefs and misguided assumptions with an honest, healthy and nurturing reality check.

Patterns of parenting: a rerun of your history?

An important part of re-evaluating what happened and de-junking judgements, includes considering our lives before we had children. We also need to reflect upon our lives *as* children, as it is part of the human condition to repeat patterns of how we were parented. Sometimes these inner templates are unconsciously repeated and other times we are aware of our own childhood suffering and are determined that for our children, things will be different—and so the pendulum can swing the other way. The experiences we had as children with our parents is, however, often mirrored in how we are as parents.

Some mothers apart have experienced difficult childhoods and have, in particular, either felt unmothered to some degree by their mothers, or have felt a lack of nurturing, being caring for, nourished, protected, cherished and all the behaviour we associate with mothering during their upbringing.

To acknowledge that you have recreated a rift or estrangement that occurred in your childhood with your children begins to break the cycle.

'My parents weren't happy together. My father was an accountant and worked long hours. I think he stayed away from home mainly to avoid my mother, who had a drink problem. Life at home was chaotic and as my father wasn't around much (and when

he was, he was angry with my mother) I took on the role of looking after everybody—as the oldest child it was my job. I tried to please my parents by being good and helpful and doing well at school. I tried so hard to control things so that people wouldn't see how crazy our family was. Trying to be in control is an illusion of course, when you live with an alcoholic. They're the one who calls the shots. Looking back, I can see that it was convenient to my father that I just got on with it. I had to grow up so quickly, and have very little sense of being mothered. In fact, I mothered my mother.'

Helen

'I was adopted and although my adoptive mother cared for us well in a physical way— she is a stoic, practical woman—she wasn't very warm towards us. I knew that she wasn't my birth mother from an early age, but it never felt right to talk to her about it or ask questions. Maybe this was because she couldn't have her own children, I don't really know. I wanted to be a good mother to my daughter and I certainly never imagined that I'd leave her, not after I'd been left.'

Elaine

'This feeling of darkness, abandonment and silence has kept haunting me all through my life. As I grew up I told myself I will get married, have a house full of laughing kids, summer barbeques on the patio with lots of friends and all my family. I won't ever feel lonely when I am grown up and married. My father never thought this would happen: "You will be a lonely old woman. I can't see you ever getting married. Something's wrong with you, you're mad." Everything I did he belittled—he never showed me love or affection. My husband thought I was mad too, and would periodically use his fist or words to reinforce how mad I was, and I accepted my fate.'

Carla

As a mother apart, exploring the dynamics of your childhood can have an important role in understanding why and how you are separated from your child. Just acknowledging that you felt unnurtured, unprotected or abandoned as a child will help you to see the bigger picture of patterns that repeat themselves. Recognising a past history of separation will help you to get your experience as a mother into perspective.

For some acknowledging is enough, but for others professional help from a therapist who specialises in women's issues and understands the feelings that accompany being separated from a child is necessary for healing the pain of the past. You can find out more about finding a counsellor in the Additional Sources of Help and Advice section at the end of the book.

So I urge you to consider the effects of your own childhood when writing and telling your story. By exploring the past, you'll be able to come through it and say, 'This is who I am and I am not ashamed.'

In doing this work you will be taking the first steps to healing the past, healing childhood patterns of separation.

De-junking judgements

Your judgement de-junk includes the process of writing (or if you prefer, talking into a voice recorder), rethinking your story and examining your part in it, before sharing it along with what you've lost and gained with someone you trust. But before you start your storytelling process I'd like you to press pause.

How are you feeling?

Chances are you're experiencing some degree of fear. Perhaps you fear having to face the story of your separation again, writing that part when you actually parted. I can absolutely understand that. I know. It can feel very hard. The moment of separation is often the memory that is most pain laden.

I urge not to avoid feeling this fear—to do the exercises below despite it. Although writing or telling your story might seem difficult and painful, it is an important process. When you come to read and share it with someone else, I will help you to do so in a way that is balanced and honest.

It's highly likely that when you've told your story before you've been less than fair with yourself. Perhaps you believe that you were more to blame, more responsible for the situation than you actually were.

I imagine that these feelings are to a greater or lesser degree, capable of making you sound like a selfish, bad, abandoning (or add whatever might hook you) mother. The way to confront, shrink and work through your feelings is to write and speak your story, and then reassess it with an attitude of understanding and compassion for yourself.

Let's face your fear head on, feel it and get it over with, rather than let it control you.

Out with the fear

The place to start is to write down any fears, criticisms and negative beliefs you have about revisiting how you came to live apart from your child. Include fears of finding the words and seeing them on the page, as well as about reading out your story or telling it again, even to someone you trust. The idea is that you get them all down, every last one.

Here are some possible fears:

- I will be overwhelmed by anger and rage and not be able to cope

- I will die of shame and guilt

- I will go mad

- I will find out that I really am a bad, abandoning mother

- I will start crying and never be able to stop

- My mother/father/family would disown me if they read what I'm going to write

- I'll find out that I hate … (you fill in the blank)

Fears and negative beliefs are just that—fears and beliefs—they aren't the facts. You can recognise them because they tend to predict disaster and sound exaggerated. What's more, they are likely to disregard your strengths, view negative things as inevitable and ignore the positive in situations.

You are not bad, you will not die of guilt, you will not be damaged by angry feelings or by crying just because you fear or believe that you will. You are fearful, that's all, and the reason why fears and negative beliefs feel so 'true' is that they go in for the kill. They find your weakest spot and head straight for it, so get them all out on the next page.

OUT WITH THE FEAR

Once you written your list, it's time to confront them. It's important to find the neutral-iser to counter each fear. You need to make sure your neutraliser is realistic and believ-able to you. You won't be able to manage your fears unless you go right to the heart of the internal message that holds you back.

**A tip—if there is a grain of truth in your fear message,
acknowledge it before neutralising it.**

Here are some examples:

- 🐾 'I will find out I really am a bad, abandoning mother' could be responded to like this: *'Writing my story will give me a chance to look honestly and fairly at all the factors that led to the separation. I did the best I could under very difficult circumstances.'*

- 🐾 Your response to 'I will be overwhelmed by anger' could be: *'Anger is a powerful emotion and can feel very intense. I can let the feeling wash over me without collapsing under its force.'*

- 🐾 'My mother would disown me if she read what I'm going to write' could be answered: *'Whether or not she would disown me is irrelevant—I'm not going to give it to her to read.'*

A final point before you start: don't worry if you struggle with the concept of neutralising your fears. It takes a little while to get the hang of this kind of confrontation. Just do your best, remembering to be kind to yourself. Simply acknowledge in writing that you know a fear or negative belief exists and then write 'I am daring to believe that I am not a bad mother' or 'I'm daring to believe that I won't drown in an ocean of grief and tears'. Dare and then believe it!

Strength for your journey

Please know that nothing you have done is beyond compassion, understanding and acceptance.

Not leaving your home, not leaving your partner, not leaving your child. You did whatever you did because you had to get out, or you thought it best, or it was the only way to survive and it was the best you could do at the time. Even if what you fear is true, at least you'll know, and the way forward will become clearer. To acknowledge that you left your child because you needed to discover yourself, fulfil yourself, grow up, hunker down, start a new life, end an old one—whatever the reason—will help you feel clearer within yourself and will therefore be easier for you and your child to understand.

Your story of healing

The place to start your healing process is to write a story—the story of how you came to live apart from your child.

Stage 1 – Holding up the mirror

Write the story of how you came to live apart from our child. If writing either isn't practical or doesn't appeal to you, speak your story into a voice recorder. Read the guidelines below as they will apply in principle, whether you write or record your story.

Write freely without censoring anything. Give yourself absolute permission to include everything and anyone relevant to your situation. Don't skimp by jotting down a few lines. Don't worry about spelling, grammar or needing to sound this way or that. Don't rush it. Give yourself time to connect with your feelings as you write. Give it body. Make it detailed. How long should it be? As long as it needs to be for you to feel that you told your story in full. Don't leave a stone unturned. Include:

- What you felt about certain people.

- Their actions and how they made you feel.

- What you felt about yourself then and how you feel about yourself now.

- What you did and what you failed to do.

- Reflect on your childhood. Contemplate your maternal line. Consider how you were mothered and see if you can link this to your own experiences of being a mother.

Write all the judgements lurking insider you—outer judgements from the world that you might be shamed by and inner judgements, harsh beliefs you have about yourself. Write down the things that make you feel guilty and anything that makes you feel bad about yourself. If you left, there will be reasons why you wanted to leave—completely valid reasons. Don't allow your fear of the judgement of others or yourself stop you from this process. Throw a spotlight on it all:

- Write about your pain, your anger, your mixed feelings.

🦋 Write the secret things, the heart of the matter that is hard for you to acknowledge, the things that perhaps you've never spoken about and have hidden away.

🦋 If relevant, make sure you give air to the part of you that *wanted* to leave. The part of you that wanted to leave your husband, partner, parent, lover, home, town and, yes, even your child too. Unless we acknowledge that we wanted 'out', at least in part, we risk keeping ourselves locked in guilt.

🦋 Include any self-criticism that tells you that you didn't do the best you could at the time of separation (which you jotted down earlier in the chapter).

Take your time, there's no need to rush this important work.

Well done! You've faced your fears and written your story. Have a break and take some time to appreciate yourself for being courageous and honest.

Stage 2 – The trusted friend reality check

READ YOUR STORY AS A 'TRUSTED FRIEND'

The next step is to read your story as you imagine a trusted friend would. Perhaps you have someone in mind. Let's think about the qualities of a really good friend. Some of obvious attributes are: compassion, understanding, empathy, non-judgemental, honesty, tact, loving and caring. As your own trusted friend, tap into your intuition—the soft, subtle voice of your inner wisdom. Judgements, criticisms and anxieties tend to chatter, nag or guilt-trip us quite noisily and sharply. Your intuition on the other hand, is generally a quiet but often strong 'inner knowing'. It is one of your most trustworthy guides and certainly a powerful characteristic of your inner trusted friend.

Now, making sure you're relaxed and comfortable, sit or lie down quietly for a while and imagine these and other positive qualities of a good friend flowing into you. As you breathe in, imagine each quality finding its place in your heart—one at a time. On your out breath, imagine your body releasing any fears, tension, negativity or judgement that might be lurking around inside. Take your time. Breathe each attribute into your heart and imagine your heart radiating each quality around your body.

When you are relaxed and secure in the mantle of being your own trusted friend, read or listen to your story again. As you do so, run everything past the filter of being the good friend that you have visualised inside you. Let all those good qualities soak on the page.

Now you're ready to do your trusted friend reality check.

As you read, make trusted friend notes next to, or cross out anything you've written about yourself that sounds unbalanced, unfair, judgemental, narrow minded, unrealistic or downright cruel. If you've used a voice recorder, play back your story and make notes about anything that sounds off-key. Watch for when you've reacted from a place of guilt, come across as being over responsible, denied or downplayed other people's behaviour towards you, or minimised the role others played that resulted in your separation from your child.

When you read about the behaviour of other people towards you—do a balanced and fair, trusted friend reality check. What I mean by this is put your own emotions to one side for a while, and in the position of trusted friend, ask yourself whether that person's behaviour, attitude and actions towards you were consciously menacing. Was their behaviour deliberately abusive, unkind or unjust? If they have an illness such as an alcohol or drug addition, acknowledge the illness but don't ignore or condone their behaviour towards you.

TAKE TIME TO REWRITE YOUR STORY

Bearing your trusted friend notes, changes and crossed out sections in mind, write your story again making sure it is a balanced account of what happened. If you've used a voice recorder, tell your story again to include your amendments. How much you change will depend on your level of judgement of yourself. Be gentle with yourself. Be reflective about the part others played too, but acknowledge unacceptable, bullying or abusive behaviour when it was or is so. Be as honest as possible. You're doing well. When you're ready, move on to the final stage in the process.

Stage 3 – Share your story with someone you trust

We can't heal our redundant, negative feelings alone. We need others to hear our story and help us heal ourselves. When someone we trust listens to us they validate the difficult situations we found ourselves in, the choices that were open to us and the decisions we made.

The act of telling your story honestly, and hearing what you say, will help you to clarify what you were and were not responsible for. If your boundaries and judgements are suspect or you start to waver or become confused, your listener will be able to question, reality check and present a more accurate perspective to you.

To risk and tell someone you trust something that you've never told anyone before can be a powerful, healing moment in your life.

Who will you choose? Pick someone whom you instinctively believe is wise and patient, someone who won't judge you or interrupt your flow too much. You need someone who can sit with you and feel outrage at injustices and compassion for your guilt and shame. Select somebody who can applaud your tenacity, courage and strength, someone who wants you to be successful and happy and who is capable of cheering you along in life.

If talking about your story is hard at first, give them both versions to read or let them listen to your voice recordings. Sit with them while they do this. You might feel you want to talk during or afterwards. With a bit of luck your 'listener' will respond with an open heart, which will give you courage and the words to tell your tale.

If it feels safer or more comfortable, find a counsellor who will listen to your story. Let's be very clear—the emotions connected to motherhood can be complicated and overwhelmingly intense. Reaching out for help when you need it shows great strength.

Now, give yourself credit for undertaking the exercises above. You've completed a very important step in the process of facing your fears, inner judgement and tough feelings which are a real challenge to examine and verbalise.

By reviewing your story in a balanced way and sharing it with a trusted friend, you now have a more honest and accurate account of your circumstances as a mother apart.

Journaling—your ongoing de-junk

Please consider using the uncensored writing process you used to write your story as an ongoing strategy to meet self-beliefs head on, understand them and gain a better sense of yourself. Writing freely in this way, also known as journaling, is an effective way of facilitating new awareness and change.

Getting thoughts, feelings, worries and problems down on to the page instead of being stuck in your head will help you learn more about yourself, what motivates you and can help you make properly thought through decisions about your future.

There is only one rule for journaling—to give yourself permission to write absolutely anything. Write from the heart.

Journaling can fulfil a number of positive functions:

- It can act as a salve and comfort when painful truths are uncovered.

- It can be a powerful way of releasing anger and expressing it in vivid ways that you'd choose not to act on. Expressing the full force of anger through journaling helps you to pull out the truth, sift through it to find which parts, if any, need to be said or auctioned.

- It can provide freedom from the worry that spirals frighteningly in your head. Writing thoughts down creates clarity and helps you to determine and let go of unnecessary, negative and obsessive thoughts.

- The process of writing when you feel stuck in a feeling is an excellent way to unblock. Just by writing 'I feel stuck and I don't think things will ever change', and allowing whatever else is going on in your head to free flow, shifts things. It's like just sitting in a boat and trusting the river flow will take you to the sea.

- Journaling is like having a friend on tap. Writing fears, sorrows and innermost thoughts is like having a trusted friend to hand whenever you need them.

How to get started:

CHOOSE A JOURNAL THAT FEELS SPECIAL TO YOU

Select a book that attracts you, something that is appealing and welcoming but not so expensive that it could inhibit you. A beautiful book can inspire you to write. Likewise, a dull exercise book can be off-putting, but if you personalise it by decorating the cover, it can be transformed into a journal that has significance and meaning to you. Whatever book you choose, make sure that it represents your own, special sanctuary for journaling.

FOR YOUR EYES ONLY: KEEP IT PRIVATE

Writing your journal is a solitary activity. What you write belongs to you alone. Knowing that your journal is private will give you the freedom to write whatever you think and feel. The only way to be really honest with yourself is to know that someone else isn't reading what you are writing. You have a right to privacy. If necessary, hide your journal.

KEEP AN EYE OPEN FOR EMOTIONAL UNDERSTANDING AND CHANGE

Once you relax into the process of journaling you'll find that sometimes you experience realisations as you write. At other times it's useful to go back and read what you've written previously to gain understanding. These important insights chart your personal growth and provide you with new ways of looking at the world. Be on the lookout for unexpected reactions and feelings as you write; these are clues and prompts to guide you in your relationships, choices and desires.

DARE TO DREAM

The way to begin creating the life you want for yourself is to visualise what you want and how you will look when you achieve it. Allow yourself to write down dreams, goals and ideal situations without censure or telling yourself to 'get real'. The clearer you become about what you long for, the more chance you have of creating the life you want for yourself.

WRITE ABOUT HAPPY DAYS AND POSITIVE THOUGHTS

Understanding, healing and learning isn't all about pain and difficulty. Capture simple moments of ease and comfort. Write about times when you felt good or said something you instinctively felt was right and it made a real difference. Describe beautiful moments and days that you can reread during times when you feel low. Catch flashes of insight and positive thoughts. Use coloured pens or draw to celebrate good things.

Many of the exercises in this book are specific, focused ways of facing issues relating to living apart from your child. Journaling will complement them and I hope you'll find the process a useful method for mulling over, reorganising and incorporating new insights into your life.

Before we move on, let's summarise what we've covered so far.

De-junk debrief

- Just because we live in a world of gender double standards, it doesn't mean that we are powerless in the world.

- Let your intuition be your guide. Ignore outer opinions on who and how to care for others, including your children. Turn up the volume of your voice of inner knowing as you nurture and love others.

- Keeping shameful secrets keeps us stuck. Shrink any lingering guilt and shame by reality checking and sharing with someone you trust.

- Being honest with ourselves is key to our health and well-being. By accepting that there was a part of us that needed or wanted to live apart from our child (if this is so) frees us from the distortions of shame that harm us and confuse our children.

- The way to break the cycle of broken mothering is to acknowledge and learn more about its pattern in our lives, even if it's painful. Healing the broken cycle starts with us—by treating ourselves gently and through self-acceptance.

And it's this theme of healing and acceptance that we explore further in the next chapter as we take a closer look at how to manage loss and grieving from the unique position of being a mother apart.

Chapter 3

Opening your heart to be a mother apart

'The most beautiful people we have known are those who have known defeat, known suffering, known struggle, known loss, and have found their way out of the depths. These persons have an appreciation, a sensitivity and an understanding of life that fills them with compassions, gentleness, and a deep loving concern. Beautiful people do not just happen.'

Elisabeth Kübler-Ross

Your focus in the last chapter was to look again and re-evaluate how you came to live apart from your child, to sift through the facts and your family history in order to get a genuine and compassionate picture of your personal circumstances.

In this chapter we move on to explore how to manage the feelings of loss and pain associated with separation. The experience and depth of loss from living apart from our child is unique to us as individuals. The pages that follow will show you how to find the strength and work your way through your pain by opening your heart. You will learn about the ways in which mothers apart can get stuck in the cycle of grief, along with strategies for overcoming this.

Let's start a brief exploration of loss and grief for mothers apart from their children.

Disenfranchised grief

What does this mean and how does it manifest in the lives of women who live apart from their children?

Kenneth Doka in *Disenfranchised Grief: Recognising Hidden Sorrow* describes this condition as grief that isn't openly acknowledged, mourned or publicly accepted. A person who has experienced a loss and doesn't feel they have a socially recognised right to express their grief, tends to feel alienated from society as a result. Someone who feels that they can't legitimately grieve their loss after having an affair would be one example of disenfranchised grief. Another would be a mother who chose to give up her child for adoption.

As mothers apart, unchecked external judgement from an unsympathetic world along with harsh internal judgement and unhealthy guilt can render us some of the 'hidden' grief stricken that Doka describes. Where does this leave us?

If we don't feel that our grieving is permissible, our suffering remains unrecognised, unnamed and ultimately unprocessed.

The legitimacy of suffering

We read an article about a child that has been snatched from her parents. On a television programme we hear elderly people talk about the suffering they experienced when separated from their parents during the war—sharing in excruciating detail the last day they saw them, their final farewell. This kind of loss triggers deep pain within mothers apart. Sometimes we can't bear to watch, listen or read for a moment longer—all that suffering, *through no fault of their own*. 'What right do I have to grieve?' we chastise ourselves. We have damaged our children. We have caused our own torment.

A pause for some questions: Who benefits if you tell yourself you don't have the right to feel pain and grieve?

> Does it ease any hurt your child might be feeling?
> Does it right any wrongs?
> Will it turn back the clock?
> Will it make the future turn out well?
> Does it help you or anyone else in the present?

The answer to all those questions is *no*.

To tell yourself that you don't have the right to feel bad, that you're too guilty to be allowed to grieve, serves no one.

In fact it is detrimental to everyone around us. Whether we have caused it or not, we are in pain and this needs to be addressed.

Perhaps you are reading this thinking that allowing yourself to grieve isn't something you have a problem with. It's knowing *how* to deal with your heartache that troubles you.

NO MATTER HOW GREAT OR SMALL YOU CONSIDER YOUR LOSS OF EVERYDAY MOTHERING OF YOUR CHILD TO BE, THE GRIEF YOU FEEL IS JUSTIFIED.

So how can mothers apart cope with loss and grief, living apart from her child? Is it possible to manage your grief and find acceptance of your situation?

I believe it is.

Opening your heart—the foundation of big-hearted mothering

What does this mean? It might sound like a strange idea, especially as you might have a big pull to protect yourself from current pain or painful experiences that might happen in the future.

Big-hearted mothering—opening your heart to your status as a mother apart—means that you turn to face your loss, grief or pain instead of trying to block it off, minimise it or run away from it. It means drawing on all the healthy tenacity and strength you have inside you (yes, you *are* a strong woman) and commit to opening your heart and growing bigger as a person and as a mother in order to embrace your circumstances as a mother apart instead of resisting them.

Big-hearted mothering requires different qualities to everyday mothering. It entails that you let go and hold on in equal measure. Holding on lightly but never letting go even though it feels like our heart is breaking is what we are called on to do. And as a mother apart you will feel like your heart has been broken, perhaps many times over. But loving and holding on will bring rewards—sometimes in ways we long and hope for but also in other, quite unexpected ways too.

Why open your heart? Because resistance uses up more of your energy than opening your heart and accepting the way things are right now. It's also a lot more painful to struggle and fight against. Now, I am not saying that you should give up, roll over, give in—that you shouldn't stand up for your rights. Neither am I implying that you should give up hope. What I am suggesting is that you open up your heart to avoid narrowing your outlook and your options. Resistance narrows and closes down possibilities. Opening your heart gives you more room to live fully and love others more deeply—and most importantly, to love yourself.

Big-hearted mothering entails creating a place of refuge, peace, acceptance and serenity within yourself.

The heart is the centre of the body, the core of our being. The art of big-hearted mothering needs to be learnt from the inside out. It's not something you put on or pull over yourself, rather it's a process that requires an internal focus. As you discover

and widen this capacity within you, you will find a growing acceptance of your status as a mother apart—that you can bear it, that you do have the strength. Think of opening your heart as exercising an underdeveloped muscle. It might be hard at first, and hurt a bit too, but with regular practice, you'll get stronger and it will become easier.

By opening your heart, you'll create a way of being that you can depend upon and which will guide you—an assuredness, a confidence that comes from knowing that you are a good woman who is capable of loving deeply and unconditionally.

In holding this place inside you, you will reap the rewards of coming home to yourself, relying on your instincts to guide you and your ability to love no matter who says what, whether your child shows you love in return, or indeed whether or not you see her or him. By opening your heart, you will have a place of comfort and sustenance in your life that will always be there, day and night, whether you're with others or alone.

I don't for one minute pretend that any of this is necessarily easy. It takes courage.

It is not instant. It takes practice. And it is deep work. Inside out work isn't about quick fixes, putting a brave face on it or strapping on a suit of armour. It means a decision to face your feelings, the extent of your loss—slowly, consciously and honestly—and through opening your heart to the process you will find a growing acceptance for your situation and the uncertainty that goes with it.

Here are some supportive strategies and attitudes that you can develop to help increase your self-belief and sustain you as you practise big-hearted mothering:

- Although you might feel like a hapless victim, please believe that you aren't being punished. You have the opportunity to learn and grow from a unique experience. In that sense, your greatest wound is your greatest gift.

- We can't see the bigger picture of life. Work at letting go of trying to control what you *can* change. What you *can* change is yourself, so concentrate instead on increasing awareness of yourself and growing into all you can be as the amazing, unique and special individual that you are.

- Allow yourself to be the authentic you and make a commitment to accept yourself for who you are. Forget perfection. Make being a good enough mother the focus of your attention.

- Direct your energy to ensure that you replace judgement of others with tolerance, empathy and understanding, even though you might not agree with them.

🍃 Even though it's the challenge of a lifetime try, little by little, to foster a presence of grace, dignity, compassion and patience. These qualities go a long way in neutralising spite, revenge, possession and jealousy—in us and other people.

I want to make it really clear: although facing the reality of your situation can be painful, big-hearted mothering is not about turning into a martyr or having to endure suffering above and beyond because you are a mother apart.

It isn't pain and misery that underpins big-hearted mothering but rather the reverse—loving. Loving yourself, loving your child, loving people close to you and generally, having a loving intention for all those around you.

**The more you practise big-hearted mothering, the easier it will be
to access inside you—and to return to.**

Now, I'm not saying that everything in your life will turn into 'happily ever after'. It's unrealistic to expect that you'll never hurt, doubt, be in conflict or feel lost. Things don't always work out the way we want. You will also have days when you dip in and out of your resting place—shifting from pain and struggle to allowing and acceptance. That's OK. That's how life is because we are human. You can learn to roll with uncertainty and the hard times, to keep open and flexible, and bend with instead of tensing up and snapping through resistance. When you're stressed, coming back to the core of you is harder but all the more important. As you work on bringing yourself back to accepting yourself and what is in your power to change, you will find it easier to right yourself if others blow you off course.

THE MORE YOU WALK ALONG THE PATH OF OPENNESS AND ACCEPTANCE THE WIDER IT WILL BECOME. WITH REGULAR USE, A NARROW PATH WILL BECOME A WELL-WORN ROAD, MAKING FOR AN EASIER JOURNEY. IN TIME, ACCEPTANCE AND BIG-HEARTED MOTHERING WILL BEGIN TO SUSTAIN YOU.

It will also sustain your relationship with your child as she comes and goes. Big-hearted mothering will mean that you are ready for a reunion at any time. Who knows what's around the corner? Whatever the future holds, you will be sustaining yourself and loving deeply from a distance, doing your best with an honest, clear and open heart, and that will not go to waste. Big-hearted mothering is about growth and increase, rather than shying away, closing down or hiding—reflecting, accepting and connecting will bring other gifts into your life too.

The grief cycle

It isn't my intention to downplay in any way the terrible losses that some people suffer—the death of a child, the suicide of a relative, the murder of someone they love. But as traumatic as these awful circumstances are, there is a devastating but permanent reality—the person who is loved and cherished is dead. This means that even if a bereaved person becomes overwhelmed by their feelings or is stuck in a stage of grief—for example, denial or anger—with help and with the passing of time, the loss can be grieved for and healing can begin. Whether you have fairly regular contact or none at all—if you are in pain, suffering the loss of not being able to mother as much as you would like—the chances are high that you are stuck in the grief cycle.

So what is a grief cycle and in what ways do mothers apart become stuck in it?

Through her work studying terminally ill patients, psychiatrist Dr Elisabeth Kübler-Ross observed what she called the 'Five Stages of Grief' as being the common process people go through as they are face death or tragedy. These stages—each an emotional response— are now recognised as being true for us as we face many types of painful, life-changing situations.

Grief and loss is a unique process. Our personality type and the severity of the circumstances we face will determine our experience of the loss. In a nutshell, the stages of grief can be regarded as a roller coaster ride of emotions we will go through when we experience loss. They are:

Denial – After the initial shock of a traumatic experience, denial is usually the first stage in the grief process. Feeling numb, we might carry on as if nothing has happened. There is a sense of disbelief: 'This can't be happening to me'.

Anger – Anger can be expressed in ways that are familiar to us but we can also experience uncharacteristic outpourings of rage about the loss and blame other people in an attempt to stop feeling overwhelmed. It's usual to ask 'Why is this happening to me?' which can also mean 'Why isn't it happening to you?'

Bargaining – As anger subsides, the desperation of 'bargaining' begins. We try to come up with ways to get back what we've lost. 'If only I hadn't …' or 'I promise I'll … if you …' are common bargaining pleas. We cling to the hope that what has happened can be reversed.

Depression – The next stage is usually a slump into depression, which isn't a sign of mental illness but rather a response to loss. We realise that the loss is real. We cry and sometimes withdraw from others. There is a deep sadness and a sense of helplessness and hopelessness. No prospects or happiness can be seen beyond what we've lost.

Acceptance – This is the point at which we have adjusted to the loss and are able to move on with our lives. It includes taking responsibility for ourselves and our actions. This doesn't mean that we don't feel sadness about the loss again. Anniversaries of the event and special dates can stir up strong feelings. Over time, the severity of the loss subsides, but in some cases may never go away entirely.

Before reaching acceptance, we usually move back and forward through the other four stages as we come to terms with our loss, making the five stages into a cycle.

Even if the idea of grieving isn't something that instantly resonates with you, understanding the different stages of the cycle and how they might play out in your life will help you through the ups and downs of being a mother apart. Knowing that we go through a process of loss and grief can be comforting and reassuring, even if what triggers it appears to be relatively minor.

How deeply you will experience the grief cycle will depend on how great the separation or loss of your child feels to you. If you are a mother apart who has regular, frequent contact with your child and you regard yourself more of a non-resident co-parent, you are less likely to go through an intense grieving process for the loss of your child, but there might be times when you feel the loss of not being an everyday parent or when the reality of your life as a parent falls short of what you might consider the ideal family environment in which to raise your child.

Mothers with little or no contact on the other hand face a major challenge. The nature of our loss, a child that lives elsewhere, means that we are at risk of becoming stuck in the grieving process. Our child is alive—we are still deeply attached to her or him and because of this the process is never truly completed.

Whatever the level of contact you have with your child it *is* possible to understand the nature of your experience of loss and grief and find healthy, constructive ways of working through your feelings—and this is what we will be exploring in the rest of this chapter.

Grieving as the journey, not the end destination

To help you find what you need, I have separated our search into the grief cycle into two sections.

The section that follows immediately, '*A mother with no contact—falling down the trapdoor of denial*', is for you if have no contact with your child.

If you have contact with your child you may still find this section useful to you. However you are likely to find what you need in the next section called *'A mother with contact— when the circle becomes a square'*.

A MOTHER WITH NO CONTACT—FALLING DOWN THE TRAPDOOR OF DENIAL, AND HOW YOU CAN HELP YOURSELF OUT

If a mother has no contact at all, reaching the acceptance stage—which would allow her to move on with her life in a healthy way—is difficult because she knows that the child is in the world without her and part of her at least will be living in hope that this will change—that someday there will be a reconnection.

For others, consciously keeping even the smallest hope of a change is too painful.

> *'I've been fighting what seems like a losing battle for years, going to court, trying to get contact. The mistakes I made, my ex making the past sound even worse than it was, the children's rejection of me. I don't let myself daydream about a happy ending. It's just not going to happen.'*
>
> *Jayne*

Sometimes, especially when children are very young, it might seem less painful to tell yourself 'never' than thinking about the reality—the potential loss of all those child-hood years, which could change suddenly or slowly over a number of months, or in the long term in the form of an adult–child reunion.

To say that you have given up hope of ever being reunited with your child is an indication that you are in denial because no one knows what the future might bring. It might feel as if things will never change, but in reality change is the only thing we can be certain of. Children have turned up on doorsteps out of the blue, never to return from where they have come.

To tell yourself that it's just not going to happen as Jayne above has is a way of protecting yourself. Now, this strategy will go some way towards allowing you to cope and carry on with life—and, my goodness, if this is true for you then give yourself credit for finding a way of shielding yourself, for stopping yourself from going under. But taking this stance is still denial—and when you deny something to yourself, you begin to lose your grasp on reality and life will become distorted, one way or another. Possibilities for healing and growth narrow and can close down.

It is with absolute sincerity and the highest regard for your situation that I offer the following suggestions.

With gentle honesty, ask yourself the following questions:

- Are you keeping yourself stuck in denial by giving up on there ever being any change to your circumstances?

- Are you resisting and fighting the legal or social care system, or other people too hard and for too long, to the detriment of your health?

- Do you imagine that contact with your child would solve all of your problems?

All of these beliefs along with others are understandable defence mechanisms which can work for a while but which will ultimately block you from your feelings and a chance to accept, heal and move on.

A MOTHER WITH CONTACT—WHEN THE CIRCLE BECOMES A SQUARE

STUCK IN DENIAL

If you are a mother with some or regular contact it is likely you'll experience slipping backward and forward through the first four stages as your child comes in and out of your life. Sometimes this takes the form of going through an incomplete cycle on a regular basis over many years. Here's one mother's experience:

> *'In the weeks leading up to the school holidays when my children come to stay, I spend a lot of time planning the things we're going to do together. Days out, but also just being at home together doing ordinary everyday things. I look forward to seeing them so much and when they're here I start to hope that things will change and they'll stay. It doesn't sound good but I imagine what I'd do or say if they told me they weren't happy living with their father. I find it hard to hear that they're happy with him and I sometimes feel I'm competing, like I'm trying to win them over, showing them what a great time we could have if we were together again. Then when they go I feel exhausted and so, so low. Like it's hopeless and what's the point?'*
>
> *Natalie*

By relating Natalie's experience to the grief cycle we can see that she slips into denial even before her children arrive. In the excitement of making plans for the holiday she begins to build up a hope that this time they'll come to her and not return to their father. Because she's built her hopes up she begins to feel frustrated and angry when she sees that nothing's changed, that the children are settled with their father. Natalie feels bad about feeling like she does and as the pressure builds up in her, she moves into bargaining—her 'trying to win them over'. When they return home to their father she slips into a depression, crying and feeling a sense of hopelessness, that her future is bleak and meaningless.

If you relate to Natalie's story, you'll be able to see how it's possible to get caught up in a square that is never circled, a four-cornered trap that offers no release or opportunity for moving on. Some mothers apart shift around the first four stages—denial, anger, bargaining and depression—or get trapped in one stage for years. A mother with contact's experience of the denial stage can be similar to that of a mother without contact and include: fantasies of having a 'perfect' time together during which everyone is constantly happy, ignoring the fact that a child has a good relationship with an ex-husband's new wife, expecting a child to be and behave exactly as she did before the separation. In essence, the stage of denial is characterised by a lack of acceptance that things have changed.

Ways that mothers apart get stuck in stage one: denial

- Giving up hope altogether—as a form of protection

- Resisting, struggling and fighting others and the legal system too hard and for too long, to the detriment of your health and well-being

- Believing that all your problems will be solved, that everything in life will get better if only you had contact with your child

- Slipping into the fantasy of mother–child relationship—how it 'should be' or how it was before separation—resulting in a conflict with reality

STUCK IN ANGER

Getting stuck in anger might take the form of exhausting outpourings of fury or resentment or it might mean being trapped under a layer of repression if the anger is bottled up inside.

Anger can feel like something we can get our teeth into. It stops us from floundering. The trouble is that holding on to anger at our ex-partner, raging at the injustices of life in general, blaming others and holding on to bitterness, all take us away from feeling our pain. Anger can also mask our unprocessed guilt and shame. And underneath anger is fear—fear of rejection, abandonment, judgement from others, from feeling the pain of our loss.

Getting stuck in the anger stage increases your chances of adopting angry behaviour as a default position from which you attack others before they have a chance to do one over on you.

It's not uncommon for mothers apart to choose anger as a defence against feeling powerless or like a victim, especially if they've experienced physical or emotional abuse within their relationship, when they were a child or both.

Now just to be clear, to feel angry is normal and healthy. It tells us that we need to take care of ourselves. But sometimes victims of abuse find that they feel a huge amount of anger when they leave the relationship. Anger that has been pent up, sometimes for years, begins to come out as rage. Feeling a huge surge of anger to a minor, everyday trigger is usually an indicator of old anger. Anger from the past feels too big for the present.

Being aware that we're releasing old anger and at the same time expressing our anger appropriately and asking for what we need, are part of the process of coming to terms with the past. If your anger feels overpowering or frightens you or others, please get support from a counsellor. As we face the wounds of our past, our anger subsides to become a normal emotional response.

Here are some tips to help you through if you are feeling stuck in anger. Tell yourself:

- Anger is an emotion that I feel. It's energy in my body that I have control over and can choose to express calmly.

- I'm going to take time out; I don't have to respond to anyone straight away.

- There's no point in wasting my energy arguing and I refuse to let myself become resentful.

Actions for dealing with anger include:

- Learn assertive behaviour to replace aggressive acting out (see the section on boundary setting in the next chapter).

- Become curious about feeling angry and take responsibility for your own feelings and actions to avoid blaming others.

- Try to imagine the other side of the story. By 'putting yourself in someone else's shoes' and imagining what they're thinking and feeling, or by choosing to envisage an innocent or unemotional reason for something happening, will help you gain a better perspective and shrink your anger.

Following anger is the stage of bargaining—of trying to gain control and reverse reality. When we're in the bargaining stage we act from a place inside that fears and can't bear feeling helpless.

Ways that mothers apart get stuck in stage two: anger

- Pushing people away with angry outbursts

- Anger is your first response—you find yourself lashing out before you've had time to think things through

- Growing increasingly bitter and resentful

- Having a sense of that you're 'letting off steam' which can be followed by wishing that you hadn't acted or said things in anger

- Burning up inside from holding back on anger—feeling a seething rage

- Feeling that your anger gives you a sense of power and control over others

- Believing that the only way to survive is to always be on your guard and fighting back

STUCK IN BARGAINING

If you're feeling stuck in the bargaining stage, here are some suggestions to help you:

- Watch out for a sense of urgency or desperation when you're with your child. These feelings can indicate a slip into the bargaining stage. Take a deep breath, relax, let go of any panic, focus on your dignity and status as a mother and practise patience and big-hearted mothering over time.

- Try to ease any panic or sense of being overwhelmed by taking a step back and viewing 'bargaining' thoughts as your way of dealing with stress.

- Tell yourself that bargaining is a natural response, that it provides a comfort for things you can't control. Bargaining can help you 'frame' your sense of loss, making it more understandable to you. It might also be your way of coping with sadness, of helping you to avoid a downward turn into deep depression.

- Write down your thoughts before taking any action. Ask a trusted friend to reality check any bargaining thoughts. That way you'll protect yourself from making a deal that isn't in your best interests, that you might regret later.

Ways that mothers apart get stuck in stage three: bargaining

- Continuing to resist accepting the reality of the separation and trying to find ways of reversing the change.

- Trying to strike a bargain or make a deal, for example: with a child, trying subtle and not so subtle ways to persuade her to visit more often; with an ex-partner for a reconciliation out desperation rather than what is right for all concerned; with God to turn back the clock in exchange for becoming a better person.

- Repeatedly thinking and saying 'If only...' If only I hadn't done or said this, I might have persuaded the children to live with me. If only I knew then what I know now, I wouldn't have become the main breadwinner. If only I'd got help earlier, I wouldn't be a mother apart now.

STUCK IN DEPRESSION

Being marooned in the depression stage leaves you cut off from others, withdrawn from ourselves and others. Unprocessed, too much time in this stage can lead to serious mental health problems.

Here are some practical solutions to help you through if you are feeling stuck in depression:

Talk to someone. Talking helps you gain a clearer perspective on your feelings and it also helps you escape the hamster wheel effect of repetitive negative thoughts. Having a one-to-one bolsters your self-esteem too, because when someone really listens to you it lets you know you are worthy and valued.

Make a conscious effort to relax. Depression is also linked to feeling stressed, tense and anxious. Find ways of de-stressing that work for you, whether it's yoga, walking on the beach, using aromatherapy oils or having a massage.

Read. A good book can keep you company at any time of day or night and even in the bath. Old favourites can act as good friends but try new topics as well, as they could be the beginning of some new interests. Reading poetry aloud can help you to express yourself and be of great comfort too.

Listen to music. Or make music if you're able to play an instrument (and it's never too late to learn). Like poetry, music can see you through some hard times and singing along and dancing can be a healthy physical release.

Cry. You might fear that you'll drown in your tears but you won't. Crying is a fundamental part of grieving and healing. Letting your tears fall and having a good sob can discharge an enormous amount of tension, helping you to sleep more soundly and let go of painful thoughts.

Get ANGRY! Depression is anger turned in on yourself. Allowing yourself to express anger is an effective way of moving out of depression. Find the best way for you. If the thought of getting angry frightens you, try journaling about it. Having someone we trust witness how angry we feel about another person or situation can create a powerful internal shift.

Please read this if you're feeling very depressed ...

When our feelings of loss are not expressed or explored they can lead to more severe forms of depression, such as clinical depression. If your feelings of depression are making it hard for you to cope, get through the day, or lead you to feel desperate about your life or suicidal—please find help for yourself straight away. Your GP is a good place to start, as she or he will be able to assess your symptoms and refer you to another health care professional if necessary. Various mental health organisations offer information and advice, of which Mind is particularly helpful (www.mind.org.uk). Also see the Additional Sources of Help and Advice at the end of the book.

It's important to bear in mind that there aren't any quick fixes to life's problems, especially those faced by mothers apart. Coming to terms with your feelings takes time and hard work. Try to remember that although you might feel very low in energy, your situation will improve more quickly if you take an active role in working through your feelings.

Ways that mothers apart get stuck in stage four: depression

- 🐾 Withdrawing from the world, not telling anyone how you feel—believing that no one will understand or be able to help you

- 🐾 Losing all hope for future happiness—feeling resigned to your fate with a heavy heart

- 🐾 Feeling weak, very tired, ineffective and powerless

- 🐾 Feeling stuck, immobilised by the situation—feeling like lead

- 🐾 Experiencing bouts of weeping and pain, and periods of feeling nothing at all

- 🐾 Feeling sick and tired of feeling sick and tired

HOW A MOTHER APART WITHOUT CONTACT CAN REACH STAGE FIVE: ACCEPTANCE

Open your heart to the entire grief process. Allow yourself to face and feel the loss of your child. Try to keep your focus on how things are today without imagining how they will be in the future. No one knows what tomorrow might bring. Remember that you are grieving the loss of your child in your life for today—you are not completely letting go or trying to work through and 'get over' your loss. Be aware that the loss of your child might trigger memories of other major losses in your life. You might be conscious of what these are but equally you could find yourself grieving over a loss that has been forgotten or you haven't been aware of before now.

Hold a place of hope in your heart. Grieving your loss and staying open means choosing healthy hope rather than false hope.

Healthy hope is:

- 🐾 Being honest with yourself about your circumstances, and not slipping into denial.

🐾 Embracing the process. Feeling all that you feel about your loss as it is in the present.

🐾 Staying open to the possibility of change.

Staying open to change requires big-hearted mothering.

At times it will feel hard but know that this way is grounded in reality—it has meaning and possibility. This is what having healthy hope means. To remain in denial is to have false hope. It will distance you from reality and you will waste precious energy resisting the truth.

Be gentle with yourself and ask for help when you need it.

Use journaling as a process to facilitate your feelings of grief. You don't have to struggle on your own. Grieving is deep work and finding someone you trust to share your feelings with could help you to validate and come to terms with your loss.

HOW A MOTHER WITH CONTACT CAN REACH STAGE FIVE: ACCEPTANCE

Expect to go through the entire grief cycle, to a greater or lesser degree, every time you see your child.

🐾 Start by reminding yourself of the stages you can expect before they arrive. If you find yourself drifting off into a fantasy (denial) of what might have changed or of your child loving you in a way that meets your expectations, you can learn to check yourself and ground the visit in reality. For example, you can say to yourself, 'As things stand right now, Lisa will be returning to her father' or 'I accept and love Jake without any particular expectations'.

🐾 Expect to go through each stage of the cycle, and also jump back and forth between stages at times.

🐾 Keeping a journal of your feelings, writing observations down as you go along will help you as you chart your course.

Allow yourself to feel your feelings. Remember that feeling is not the same as acting them out. Phoning up your ex-partner on the spur of the moment to vent your fury would probably be acting out. Use the strategies for dealing with anger and depression above.

Embrace the grieving process. Opening your heart and practising big-hearted mothering means allowing yourself to feel whatever your feel, which includes feeling like your heart has been broken again and again. Because dear reader, it will be. I understand that this is difficult to hear—but to expect it, accept it and take good care of yourself is much, much easier than distorting reality by trying to avoid it, deny it or control it.

Take good care of yourself. Make a conscious effort not to do too much, to treat yourself with compassion and to allow yourself enough 'me time'. Getting an adequate amount of sleep, asking for support and planning fun time are all absolutely vital.

Whether you are a mother apart with or without contact, grieve as long, hard and as often as you need.

Remember that big-hearted mothering underpins a healthy, positive and growthful attitude towards living apart from your child. This attitude and approach will be mirrored in the chapters that follow, as we explore living with all that mothering apart brings your way.

Right now though, it's time to move on and we'll be doing so with dignity and a really big confidence boost in the next chapter.

Chapter 4

Moving on with dignity

What we've covered so far has been a necessary exploration of what has happened in the past in order to pave the way for living peacefully in the here and now. Let's take stock.

By now you have a better understanding of how mothers apart are affected by stereo types of motherhood, and how you might allow yourself to be hurt through external and internal judgements. You've de-junked these judgements by writing and reality checking 'Your Story of Healing' and you've then learnt about big-hearted mothering—how to open your heart to be a mother apart in order to be at peace with yourself. You know too about the importance of allowing yourself to grieve your loss as a full-time mother without getting stuck in the process or sanctioning yourself.

Now it's time to move on … and you can do so with strength and dignity.

The pages that follow will give you the tools to help you create a happy and positive future. In no particular order (you'll know which ones are of most importance to you), here are the eight mother apart confidence boosters.

The eight mother apart confidence boosters

Boost number 1: Daring to drop disaster thinking

'The horror of that moment,' the King said, 'I shall never, never forget.'
'You will, though,' said the Queen, 'if you don't make a memorandum of it.'

Through the Looking Glass—Lewis Carroll

Holding on to the horror of the moment is different to feeling the pain as we consciously process guilt and shame or work through the grief cycle. What I mean here is the habit-forming slump into panic or despair as we react to events that happen in our lives.

Living as a mother apart can be all consuming. We replay conversations with our ex-partner, our solicitor and the court welfare officer. We relive the last conversation we had with our child. We can't stop thinking about whether she or he is being cared for properly, whether they are crying for us. We obsess over the past—wishing we could turn back the clock to change what has been. We project ourselves into the future, fighting imagined horrors of what might happen next.

Our fears and fantasies control us. We let the drama of living apart from our child dominate our lives.

Why do we 'live the drama'? Fear, compulsion, guilt, self-punishment, low self-worth, trying to find control, because we've been doing it for so long now we're addicted to it—the reasons are many and varied.

What does it do to us? It keeps us on a knife's edge, keyed up, in a panic, on our guard, hypersensitive, overreactive, overwrought. It makes us ill—emotionally, spiritually, physically.

Can we stop? Yes.

How? By teaching yourself to unhook and let go. By allowing yourself, others and life in general just to be.

I grant you, it isn't easy to walk away from living the drama. It takes determination and practice to choose serenity over gut wrenching anxiety. But I promise that you will feel so much better if you do and, without a doubt, all the people that you love will benefit just as much too.

DROP THE DRAMA EXERCISE

Write down *who* or *what* triggers disaster thinking in you—for example, your ex-partner phoning to say that he wants to pick up your child earlier than usual or perhaps Sunday evenings when you feel most alone.

Reflect on how you react. What is your particular 'drama' behaviour? For example—obsessive disaster thinking, lashing out at someone else, withdrawing from the world.

Write a Positive Self-talk Assurance Plan to replace living the drama with healthy thinking options. Use the prompts below to help you, but remember, you know yourself better than anyone so be sure to include any personal nurturing self-talk to calm and centre yourself.

An example might be:

> *'I will ask myself "How important is it?" My goal is to remain calm so I will choose my battles wisely.'*

Or:

> *'Sunday evenings are "me time". I will listen to the music of my youth, bake a chocolate cake, sew my quilt or chill out in front of the TV (or whatever takes your fancy).'*

Here are some healthy behaviour approaches to help you replace disaster thinking with a positive approach:

- Firstly, open your heart to yourself. Have compassion. Treat yourself as gently and kindly as you would the most precious thing in the world. You *are* the most precious thing in the world.

- Commit to staying in the present—today is all you have.

- Believe that you have the strength to deal with problems if and when they come up.

- Relax—you'll know when you really need to take action. You only need to make a decision when there's a decision to be made. Don't allow yourself to knee-jerk. Very few things in life need an instant response.

- You'll know what to do by the feedback.

- Let go of trying to 'know the truth'—all that you need to know will be revealed to you.

- Let go of trying to control outcomes. Trust yourself, do your best and then let go. Who knows the true purpose of our lives or anyone else's? Who's to say that what happens won't be to your benefit or that of others?

- Give yourself permission to lighten up and have fun—you'll feel much better for it and so will people around you.

Put your Positive Self-talk Assurance Plan where you can see it and refer to it at any time you feel your serenity slipping away from you.

Dare to drop the disaster. Make a real effort to become more aware of your actions and reactions. Notice when you slide into unhealthy thinking and behaviour and take action to change it.

My earnest appeal to you: *please* be willing to stick at it. A deep or long time habit of disaster thinking takes time to unlearn. You *can* change how you think and behave. Practice and remember to tell yourself how well you're doing.

Boost number 2: Setting healthy boundaries

In order to move on, grow strong, take care of your needs and allow others to take responsibility for themselves, it's vital that you set healthy personal boundaries.

WHAT ARE PERSONAL BOUNDARIES?

Boundaries are invisible lines between you and somebody else that help you to look after yourself. They are the point at which you end and someone else begins. Having boundaries define us—our values, belief systems, experiences, thoughts and feelings. They let other people know what is and isn't acceptable to us. To set a boundary is to establish a limit about how others treat you. When we don't determine boundaries for ourselves, we allow others to set the standards for the relationship and we make ourselves vulnerable to people taking advantage of us.

WHY SHOULD YOU SET BOUNDARIES?

Boundaries are really important for protecting yourself emotionally, physically and spiritually. They make a big difference to your quality of life—how you feel about yourself and how others feel about you. Sometimes people overstep the mark because we just don't tell them what is and isn't OK for us. Being clear about your boundaries will help you to feel empowered—free to be you. You'll be more able to stand up for yourself, less guilty about letting others know what you need and better at saying no to what you don't want in your life.

WHERE DO YOU START?

The focus of change begins with you. Even though it might feel like you're asking other people to change, they are responsible for how they choose to react or adapt their behaviour, not you. Nobody else can tell you what is and isn't alright for you, although you might have inadvertently given this right away to someone else by not saying what you want or need.

Defining boundaries is all about you. The more you get to know yourself the clearer you'll be about where a boundary needs to be set. This means reflecting on how you feel about any given situation, being open to your feelings and using them as a guide. Feeling resentful, angry, taken advantage of and used are feelings that are often experienced though not setting and maintaining your boundaries. Saying what you need or want or saying 'No' can feel hard at first, especially for women. As you practise setting healthy boundaries you'll find that respecting yourself will make you more aware of respecting others. Setting boundaries is ultimately about mutual respect.

WHERE DOES BEING ASSERTIVE FIT IN?

Establishing a boundary requires that you act assertively. Being assertive is something that often confuses people. Just to be clear, being passive or non-assertive is to be submissive. It's when you don't stand up for your rights or honestly express your needs, feelings and beliefs. A non-assertive person often apologises for their feelings and actions and behaves in self-effacing ways.

Aggression on the other hand is about domination of others. It's when you dismiss other people's needs and stand up for yours in ways that infringe upon their rights.

When I lead assertiveness training workshops I always tell women to be on their guard against people who don't like their new, assertive behaviour and label it as 'aggressive' in a bid to put them 'back in their place'. It's also true that if you've been passive or non-assertive for many years, you might swing the other way and act aggressively until you find a middle road for yourself.

So what is the middle road? Being assertive means that you stand up for yourself in a way that doesn't violate someone else's rights. It also means that you express your opinions, needs, wants, feelings and beliefs in direct, honest and appropriate ways. It's about being courageous and true to yourself.

Here are some tips on how to set boundaries and stick to them:

- Start by looking within. Put the focus on you. Turn up the volume on what you need for yourself. Are you feeling angry, hurt, resentful or tired? What is your body telling you? Is your stomach churning with emotions? Has your energy dipped?

- Be as clear, specific and direct as possible. Use 'I' language: 'I think', 'I feel', 'I want'. It prevents you from blaming others. 'I' language is difficult to dispute—after all, no one knows what you think, feel or want better than you.

- Say 'yes' when you want to and 'no' when you mean no.

- Use assertive body language. Keep your voice steady and firm. Keep your head up and your body relaxed but erect. Keep your facial expression open and your jaw relaxed. Only smile when you're pleased and frown when you're angry.

- Know that other people's comments or opinions aren't the truth. Take time to think about what is true for you before agreeing or making a change.

🐾 If the other person tries to create a diversion, point it out calmly and repeat your message until you are heard.

🐾 If you meet objections, listen to the other person's point of view and repeat your message.

🐾 When you need to, ask for time out to think about your decision.

🐾 Instead of caving in to someone's anger, simply try to listen to criticism without apologising or offering to change— it often defuses someone else's anger. Sometimes just receiving unblocks a deadlock.

🐾 Remember that assertion means that your needs, feelings and beliefs are equal to those of others. Respect the rights and points of view of others even if you don't agree with them and, where possible, try to offer an alternative solution.

Be as honest as possible. Although being assertive and setting boundaries might seem scary at first, keep practising even if it provokes conflict. Being true to yourself is worth the effort. Choices become easier, communication becomes clearer and you'll feel less stressed and more alive.

Boost number 3: Saying sorry when you know you need to

Having completed all three stages of 'Your Story of Healing' in Chapter 2—writing, reality checking and sharing how you came to be separated from your child—you might feel that you need to make amends to someone. As it is commonplace for mothers apart to take too much responsibility for things that have happened to their children and families, it is important to wait until you've completed the 'Your Story of Healing' exercise before redressing anything.

Apologies and redressing of wrongs are only meaningful when they are heartfelt and honest. This means that they're not burdened with unassertive 'shoulds' or 'ought to's', prompted by fear, what someone else thinks or the desire to manipulate in any way. Having gone through the process of reality checking your story with your internal and external 'trusted friend', you'll guard against any guilty feelings being the motivator for amends.

Keeping it simple is a good rule of thumb:

🐾 Acknowledge what you did and explain why you did it.

- Acknowledge the effect it had on the person you're apologising to.

- Express your sincere regret for what you did and/or for what happened.

- Make reparation that feels right for you and the other. Maybe it's enough to say you're sorry and mean it. Perhaps this involves you changing a behaviour pattern. Remember, it will take a while to rebuild trust. It could even involve you giving back or receiving something.

The way to go about making amends is slowly, gently and gradually. It's a good idea to plan what you intend to say in advance. Be sure of what you feel and say. Think about your boundaries, being assertive, the rights and needs of the other person and your own. Words are powerful and we need to be mindful of their impact.

THE DO'S AND DON'TS OF MAKING AMENDS

- Making amends to yourself is a good place to start. Please *do* so. This chapter has ideas to help you.

- Redressing wrongs is not a punishment, so *don't* beat yourself up in the process.

- *Do* be honest about your feelings—first of all because your apology will be more truthful and meaningful, and other people will sense this. Also, saying how you feel is empowering as no one can tell you that your intent or feelings aren't true. Only you know what and how you feel.

- *Don't* make amends that will harm people or upset the lives of others. Use your intuition here—sometimes the moment has passed and or it was never something that would be possible to do. It would be better in cases like this to write the person a letter you don't send (see boost number 4). This can also be a very powerful process when you don't know where people are or if they've died.

Boost number 4: Writing a letter that you don't send

Writing a letter that won't to be received by anyone is a useful way of exploring what we believe about a person or situation. An unsent letter will allow you to express yourself freely and provide you with a chance to say exactly how you feel, right from the heart. You can write to specific people in your life—your child whom you miss, a court welfare officer who enrages you, an ex-partner who has let you down. It will help you to process and let go of conversations that took place in a way that you didn't like and lay to rest obsessive thoughts of 'If only' I had said this or that. Letter writing can also provide healing for those times when a conversation can't take place in reality, such as when the recipient is unwilling or no longer alive.

Try rewriting a letter until it truly says what you need to say and you are clear about what you feel towards the recipient, situation or object. You might choose to use the exercise as a practice run for a conversation that you decide to have in the future.

Letter writing can be a good method of self-support too. You might want to write to yourself, perhaps starting something like this:

Dear (your name), I've got so much to say about seeing Jamie again …

You might also decide to write to yourself from the place of 'wise woman' inside yourself or your 'inner therapist'. If, for example, you were having a really tough day, you could write reassuringly, reminding yourself that you'll feel better tomorrow when your mood shifts, that everyone has good and bad days.

Unsent letters can be about anything that is upsetting and confusing to you, or needs to be expressed. Even writing to an inanimate object is not as difficult as it might sound.

You might feel celebratory and excited about your new home and start your letter:

Dear wonderful, new home …

Or you might feel anger and hurt and begin with:

Dear day that I lost residency …

Writing letters that you don't send is about finding the words and new meanings to your relationships with others, events and objects. It will help you reality check your feelings and understand your choices, highlight what you don't want and gain clarity on what you need, dream of and truly want for yourself.

Boost number 5: Finding the words to talk about being a mother apart

Talking about our circumstances as mothers apart to people who don't know us can feel like a big risk. How will they react? We wonder whether they will they judge us. We sometimes try to shift the conversation on to firmer ground and away from our children.

Some of us choose a response according to who we're talking to, but generally speaking our anxiety tends to make us react in one of three ways.

Denying or lying. Without a doubt, if we lie about or deny the fact we have children, we are the people who suffer the most. As everyone knows, lies are very hard to keep track of and they often lead to other untruths, making life increasing unmanageable. But most importantly, to deny something as fundamental as having a child is to reject a vital part of us. Not talking about your rite of passage from womanhood to motherhood closes down a big piece of yourself. Both you and the world loses your experience and wisdom of sharing the mother in you.

Our deception blocks relationships with others, as intimacy requires honesty. But even more damagingly we cut ourselves off from our feelings and instincts. In our bid to protect ourselves our hearts begin to close and our world becomes distorted.

If this sounds harsh, please know that my intention is to urge you to find a way to be as real as possible as a mother apart for the sake of your well-being and those with whom you have relationships, not least your child. It is possible find the words.

Drying up. This is also a painful response. We start to talk and peter out. We feel embarrassed as we stumble over words. Sometimes we're defensive, pulling on body armour and shooting out a curt retort to what might have been an innocent enough question about our lives. Or we bow our heads and say nothing at all, which makes us isolated.

Saying too much in an attempt to make the listener understand. We find ourselves pouring it all out. Needing to explain—haphazard, unthinking, without care for ourselves, we hear ourselves saying things we didn't want to say. Each sentence requiring another to explain its predecessor, digging ourselves further into a hole, baring our souls. Talked into a corner we are exposed and vulnerable. We can't undo what we have done. Unwittingly we comprised our dignity.

WHY TELL? NEEDING TO AND WANTING TO

Getting clear about your motivation for talking about your circumstances will help you frame your response, which will broadly fall into two categories.

Needing to tell someone will usually be the need to give out information in a formal or administrative capacity. An appropriate answer needs to be factual, measured, real but unashamed.

Wanting to tell falls into the category of maintaining and developing a relationship. In order to create intimacy, friendship or love you have to show yourself, share what is in your heart. You need to divulge personal details about yourself and the other person reveals private things about themselves in turn. This self-disclosure is the cornerstone of intimacy—it requires openness and trust. And of course, it means you have to take a risk.

Let's take a minute to consider self-disclosure in a general sense.

How do you decide whether or not to take the risk of revealing yourself? It's not safe to reveal yourself to just anyone. You wouldn't usually disclose very personal things to acquaintances, colleagues, business associates. It's about what is appropriate. For example, business relationships require different levels 'professional' communication and we normally have a fairly superficial or casual level of communication with people we only know in passing.

But in order to get close to someone you need to risk, trust and reveal yourself. Disclosure shows that the other person is important to you, worthy of the investment of yourself—worth the risk. The best way to disclose personal information is for both people to do so slowly, over time, mirroring or matching the level of disclosure so that the relationship feels equal and balanced. If both people share personal details at the same level, the risk of revealing diminishes. It creates closeness and the bond that is necessary to deepen and enrich love partnerships and strong friendships.

SAY THIS OUT LOUD RIGHT NOW: 'I DON'T HAVE TO EXPLAIN, JUSTIFY OR APOLOGISE'. YOU CAN CHOOSE A CONSIDERED, HONEST, REAL RESPONSE AND THE WAY TO DO THIS IS TO BRING THE FOCUS BACK ON TO YOU—WHERE IT BELONGS.

So, how do you know what and how much to say about being a mother apart?

Most of our anxiety about sharing our lives as mothers apart tends to be connected to what other people might think, feel or do. This is in part due to unprocessed guilt and shame but it also happens when we believe that the values, opinions and feelings of others are more important than our own.

FINDING THE WORDS EXERCISE

Remember, what you reveal about yourself is your choice. The trick is to say what serves you best in the context of the conversation.

Look within yourself and ask yourself the following questions:

- What is appropriate to disclose in this relationship?

- How much does this person need to know?

- What is the value of this relationship to me?

- How much do I want to reveal?

- What do your instincts tell you about this person? Do you feel you can trust them?

- Are you able to consider talking to them based on past experience?

Now write a script, of a few sentences, for the following three categories of person: an official needing personal information, an acquaintance or casual friend, and someone you'd like to form a closer relationship with.

Pick a question that you might be asked, then formulate an answer that is comfortable for you. Here are some examples.

AN OFFICIAL NEEDING PERSONAL INFORMATION

Example question: *'Do you have any children under sixteen?'*

Example answer from you: *'I have a son who lives with his father in Norway'.*

Tips: Keep it short and sweet. This is not the same as being defensive; it's about being appropriate for the situation. The conversation would be progressed on a need to know basis. For example, the next question might be: 'How old is your son?' Your response: 'He's eleven years old'.

You don't have to feel obliged to answer any question that goes beyond the remit of the conversation. Remember your body language—head level, body relaxed. Set a boundary—all you to need say is, 'I don't feel that it's appropriate for us to discuss this'.

An acquaintance or casual friend

Example question, at a barbeque, with lots of children running around: *'Children, they're such a handful! Do you have any?'*

Example answer from you: *'Yes, I have an eleven-year-old son who lives in Norway with his father, so I don't have to deal with all this running around on a full-time basis'.*

Wait for a response. What do you feel? How much more do *you* want to say? Maintaining open and relaxed body language, continue the conversation, sharing information in a considered way, one step at a time. Take care not to overwhelm yourself or the other person by saying too much in a casual situation, where neither of you were expecting it. You can end it at any point by saying calmly, 'This isn't always easy for me to discuss, so I'd prefer not to carry on talking about it right now'. This is you taking care of your rights and needs; it's an assertive statement—not an apology.

Someone you'd like to form a closer relationship with

Example question, over a coffee: *'How did you come to be separated from your child?'*

Example answer from you: *'Well, as you can imagine, it's a complicated situation …'.*

Talk, pause and consider what you want to say next. There is no rush. Allow space for the other person to contribute too. How they respond will give you information on how much more you want to reveal. Take it a step at a time. Take care not to overwhelm yourself. Remember you aren't justifying or confessing—you are saying what happened. As with an acquaintance, it's your right to end the conversation at any time. There are advantages to pacing what you'd like to share. It gives you and the other person time to reflect. It also allows for them to match your level of disclosure in return. Mutual disclosure is what develops a relationship.

Once you've found the right words for you, practise your scripts out loud. Hearing yourself saying the words will boost your confidence. In time, what feels right will roll comfortably off your tongue.

Feedback about how confident you sound and look will help you to better prepare. Ask a trusted friend to act as someone in your script. As you role play a likely situation, you'll learn from their questions and responses and be able to fine-tune words that are true for you.

Practise in front of someone you trust or if you need extra support, find a counsellor to help you find the words.

WHAT IF SOMEONE HAS A BAD REACTION?

I don't deny that telling others that we are mothers apart is definitely a high risk disclosure. The bottom line is that you can't control the reaction of others. The good news is that you can control what you say or choose not to say.

🐾 Remember, you don't have to explain, justify or apologise.

🐾 If somebody reacts with shock or judgement it has everything to do with them and what has happened in their lives—it has nothing to do with you. You didn't make them feel anything. They felt it by themselves.

🐾 Your self-worth is not dependent on whether other people understand or empathise.

🐾 You are responsible for taking care of your needs, which might be to politely end the conversation.

🐾 Don't allow your inner critic to contribute to outside judgement.

🐾 Counter any bad experiences by nurturing yourself.

🐾 Finally, keep a bad reaction in perspective. It's just that—one individual's bad reaction. It might hurt you for a while but it need not destroy your self-esteem.

Boost number 6: Shrinking Supermother

Supermother is the arch-enemy of all women and is a particularly nasty bit of work where mothers apart are concerned. Supermother is always perfect, loving, available, says the right thing, never forgets and raises perfect children who never have any problems or struggles in life! She can just as easily be the woman on the TV in the air freshener advert as the undermining voice inside our heads.

Is there a Supermother lurking in you?
If the answer is yes, without a doubt she has to go!

These two little questions should assist: Whose approval am I seeking? What is the cost to me?

A final question to help you throw away your Supermother Lycra once and for all: If I stopped trying to meet the expectations of others, what would I do with my new found

freedom? Make sure you write down all the positives to be gained from being 'good enough' rather than perfect. For example: 'I will be more accepting of myself' or 'I'll do that scuba diving course I've always wanted to do'.

Boost number 7: Bolstering for blue days

Knowing how to look after yourself on days when life feels hard is absolutely vital. For mothers apart, difficult days can be annual occurrences like birthdays, Mother's Day, Christmas and anniversaries but they can also be the unexpected rug-pulling type, such as an angry telephone conversation or child's visit being cancelled at the last minute. Putting together a crisis management plan can be the difference between weathering the storm of sorrow or sinking to the bottom of the ocean.

On bad days it's time to go back to basics and focus on your primary human needs such as feeling safe in your own home and eating nourishing food. When life is hard, keeping things simple helps. Treat yourself with tenderness.

CREATE A BLUE DAY PAMPER PACK

Being aware of what you need to make you feel better means that you can give yourself what you need. Answer the questions below so that you can fast track first-class self-care in times of need.

- What is absolutely vital to *you* in times of crisis? For example, phoning a trusted friend, writing in your journal.

- What comforts you when you're feeling low? For example, having a warm bath, curling up in bed.

- What attention to detail would make all the difference to you in times of trouble? For example, lighting candles, keeping a little stock of comfort food, watching a favourite DVD.

A note of caution. A little of what you fancy does you good but drowning your sorrows with alcohol, numbing yourself through overeating or other drugs of choice will only make life more difficult. Please get help if you think you might have an addiction problem, if you're in danger of harming yourself or if you feel stuck in depression. There are people who care and want to help you. Please see the Additional Sources of Help and Advice section for more details.

Boost number 8: Practising the art of happiness

You have the right to be happy. No matter what has gone before or what might occur in the future, you are worthy of joy. Everything you have read in this book so far and particularly in this chapter is concerned with your happiness.

Happiness is a state of mind. You don't find happiness, you *make* happiness—and only you can make yourself happy. People close to you might try but unless you believe you deserve happiness and are willing to open yourself to joy, you will find it hard to be truly happy.

Placing conditions on your happiness such as, 'I won't be happy until my child comes to live with me' is deeply damaging for you and others. You owe it to yourself and those around you to create a fulfilling and enjoyable life, which includes letting your hair down and having fun.

Making yourself happy includes having time for yourself, good self-care, sharing life with a loving partner and friends, asking for help when you need it, finding work you enjoy, getting involved in causes that you feel strongly about. Prioritising your happiness and making it your responsibility means that your child will have a happy Mum and, whatever your circumstances, a happy mother is what your child needs now and in the future.

LAUGH OUT LOUD

Just like a good cry, laughter releases tension and anxiety. Numerous experiments show that humour dramatically reduces stress, showing significant drops in the hormones adrenalin and cortisol. Laughter is a positive, powerful medicine. I'm not suggesting that you cover up painful feelings that need to be faced but don't forget that the more you allow yourself to laugh the happier your life will be.

- What is the pay-off to you being sad, mad and unhappy? Do you ever feel guilty about feeling good?

- Is being unhappy of any benefit to your child?

- Is there anything within your control that you can change or do differently that would increase your happiness?

- Write down at least ten things that make you happy. When was the last time you experienced or enjoyed those things? When are you going to experience them again?

I hope that these eight confidence boosters, together with your reflections on Chapters 1 to 4 will champion you as a mother apart and that you will continue to find additional ways of keeping yourself strong, healthy and happy as life unfolds.

Before you move on to the next chapter you'll find a self-belief support list called Honouring Myself as a Mother Apart on the following page. You might like to photocopy this list, adding some affirmations of your own, and keep it to hand for a confidence boost any time you might need it.

Honouring myself as a mother apart

I am worthy of love and respect

I don't have to punish myself with unfair judgements or critical thoughts

I don't have to live the drama

My needs are equal to those of others; I deserve to have them met

I owe it to myself to practise outrageously good self-care

I have the right to be happy

I can let go of regret for the past and open my heart to the present and
   to what the future might bring

I am courageous. I can open myself to being a big-hearted mother apart

Chapter 5

How to exit your ex: the roadmap to conscious singlehood and creating a cooperative relationship with your ex-partner

'It's been nearly six years since I left and I still feel I'm walking on egg shells when I talk to him. Just hearing his voice makes me anxious. He's a moody person and I don't want to say the wrong thing because of what he might say about me to the kids or he might make it difficult for me to see them.'

Hayley

Physical separation is only half the process of parting from someone. The psychological bond between a couple which grows from the time of union can often take much longer to disconnect. Unconscious of this level of connection, some people remain deeply hooked into their ex for years, even when both of them are in new relationships.

Mothers apart are particularly susceptible to this, remaining bound to their ex-partner by outdated patterns of relating, guilt and fear.

Your quality of life after your divorce or separation is your choice. It might not feel this way right now if you're in the midst of an acrimonious ending or if you feel that your ex is still making your life a misery years later—but it's true.

Should *you* maintain contact with *your* ex?

Experiences of mothers apart are as wide as they are long. There are those who separate from partners who behave reasonably, taking responsibility for their actions and encouraging contact with children. Sadly there are other women who, after having a hard time within a partnership, find that their relationship with their ex deteriorates even further after they leave.

Whatever your circumstances, I encourage you to explore your part in the relationship and its downfall, dissolve your energetic connection with your ex and take stock of your emotions in order to *truly* separate and move on. This is vitally important for your health and happiness as well as the success of your next relationship, and for establishing a newly defined, workable, long-term association with your ex-partner, making it easier for you to maintain a good relationship with your child.

Does this feel impossible? If you're shaking your head and thinking, 'There's just no way that I'll ever be able to have a civilised conversation let alone relationship with my ex, not after all that he's put me through!' please carry on reading.

I want to bring the focus back on you. If your sights are locked on someone else's bad mouthing or ill-treatment you are putting your power, your future happiness in their hands.

Remember the goal: your personal happiness *and* the development of reasonable relations with your ex for the sake of your current and long term relationship with and well-being of your child.

Finding ways to remain in contact with your child via your ex-partner—which might include support from or via external sources—is worth it, *even if* he drives you crazy and you wish you never had to see him again. *Even if* you might not feel confident or assertive enough right now. *Even if,* and I don't say this lightly, your relationship was an abusive one.

What constitutes domestic violence?

Domestic violence is physical, psychological, sexual, spiritual or financial violence that takes place within an intimate relationship and takes the form of controlling and intimidating behaviour.

> 'He became more and more bullying and intimidating. I knew the way he treated me wasn't right. As I became more sure of myself, he became angrier; he knew he was losing control of me. I say that I left but I didn't—I ran away. It was the only way.'
>
> *Hayley*

'He was completely unreasonable—he would go crazy. He threatened my new partner with a knife.'

Danielle

'I was shocked and still am at the things he told our children and other people about me. Of course we had our differences and I'm not saying I was blameless, but I can't believe that he is so vindictive that he spreads lies about me. He has a strong personality and people don't know what he was like to live with. To the world he's Mr Niceguy. It's bad enough to think that people we know think I'm a real bitch, but my own children—it's too much.'

Jayne

'My self-esteem was at its lowest ever level. I had continually been told that I was stupid and totally reliant on other people and had no strengths on my own.'

Cindy

(A mother apart who is confined to a wheelchair with multiple sclerosis)

Many women who have suffered from domestic violence say that emotional abuse is more destructive and cruel and takes longer to recover from than physical abuse. Ten separate domestic violence prevalence studies conducted recently had consistent findings: one in four women experience domestic violence over their lifetimes and between six and ten women suffer domestic violence in a given year (Council of Europe 2002 and Women's Aid).

The signs of domestic violence are many and varied and range from criticism and verbal abuse (shouting, accusing, mocking), pressure tactics (withholding money, sulking, denying access to the car or phone), disrespect, breaking trust, isolating you (preventing you from seeing family and friends), harassment, threats, physical and sexual violence, and denial that the abuse happens—saying you caused it, being 'nice' in public and abusive at home, begging for forgiveness and saying that it won't happen again.

Domestic violence happens during a relationship and also after a relationship has ended.

The psychological and physical dangers of abusive relationships are severe. It can take a long time and specialist help to recover from the damage caused by domestic violence. Please find the help you need to heal unresolved issues and battered self-worth and develop your confidence to claim your rights as a woman and a mother. The Additional Sources of Help and Advice at the back of the book will point you in the right direction.

If any of above experiences of mothers apart ring true for you I am sincerely sorry and absolutely outraged in equal measure. No one has the right to bully, intimidate or deform your character. In addition to finding additional support if you need it, I encourage you to try the exercises that follow. They are designed with your well-being in mind, to help you move on with greater personal insight.

Successful singlehood: how to learn from the past and go solo with confidence

Even if you've lived apart from your ex-partner for some time, why not read through this section. You might find some useful tips to help detach yourself completely and embrace post-separation life more fully.

Letting go of blame

To heal and move on means that we have to take responsibility for our emotions and our actions. Even though it might seem entirely justifiable, to blame your ex for what he did or didn't do is to hand over your freedom. Your mood, outlook and future will be set by his past behaviour and what he might do in the future. To blame is to dodge responsibility. To take responsibility is learn and grow emotionally. *Don't wait until he changes—let it start with you.* You deserve better than to keep yourself emotionally entangled with someone you no longer live with.

Ask yourself: How does blaming my ex-partner keep me stuck in the unhappy past? Do I dwell on the bad times? Do I hurt myself all over again by remembering how mean/lazy/selfish and so on, he was?

What is the payoff? Does blaming him make me feel better, more powerful or in control? Is blaming him easier than looking at the part I played in our relationship, its downfall and even in life right now?

Imagine how much freer you would feel if you stopped blaming him. Think about how you could use this spare capacity to nurture yourself.

WHAT'S YOURS IS MINE EXERCISE

Write down what attracted you to your partner. Could it be that he was a bit of a risk taker, creative, independent, stable, a man who knew his own mind, outgoing, a strong and silent type or someone determined to have a good time?

Make a note of everything that drew you to him. It doesn't matter if those qualities turned out to be what drove you crazy in the long run. For example: a risk taker could end up jeopardising your security, someone who is independent might exclude you from a lot in his life, knowing his own mind could have meant that he domineered others with his opinion on how things were done, a strong and silent type might turn out to be cold and withholding, and someone determined to have a good time could mean that he sought pleasure for himself without a care for other people's needs.

What attracted you originally—whether or not you still like those parts of him— are typically the qualities, attitudes or abilities that you wanted for yourself. They are the unconscious parts of yourself that you yearned for, the parts you didn't own at the time—and perhaps not even now.

Make a tick next to each of the qualities that are still important to you.

Now ask yourself how well you are meeting these needs for yourself. For example:

- Are you developing the creative side of yourself?

- Have you created the stability you need?

- Do you have enough fun?

- Are you able to take the risks needed to achieve what you want in your life?

- What else do you want to develop in your life?

CREATE A 'NEEDS' TO-DO LIST

Write down a positive action that you will take for each need that is important to you. Then put a date by when you will get the ball rolling to meet each need. Make it realistic. Having a timeframe isn't there to add pressure in your life—it's there to make sure you give yourself what you need.

Being conscious of the negative side of what attracts you can lessen the likelihood of making the same mistake in future relationships. It will also help you understand the dynamics of your relationship with your ex-partner and by acknowledging the message within your attraction, you will be better able to let go of pain, anger and resentment at some of his behaviour.

It works in reverse too: what unconscious qualities do you think your ex fell for in you?

As much as we might not like it, two people make up the dynamics of every relationship.

Walk in his shoes for a while

Although this might be a challenge, this 'view from the opposite side' exercise will help redefine your relationship. Remember that you're trying this exercise for *your* sake—you don't have to clomp around in his shoes forever.

- Consider the ways your ex behaved towards you that caused you to feel bad, upset you or made you angry.

- What do you think his experience was? Imagine his side of the story. What do you think he felt?

- Does he still act this way towards you? What could you do differently to lessen the likelihood of hooking those feelings and actions in him now? This isn't the same as cowtailing or giving in to his bad behaviour. It means taking a fresh look at how you behave and seeing whether there's a more constructive way of doing things.

The only person you can change is you. If you change how you behave the energy between you and other people changes too.

Remember violence and abusive behaviour is unacceptable, whatever his upbringing or background. However, understanding how he might feel can help you decide on how to change how you relate to him.

RECLAIMING YOUR LIFE EXERCISE

ARE YOU READY?

Healing, moving on and feeling optimistic about the future takes time. The more venomous the divorce, the longer the recovery period. As many mothers apart usually experience a long and difficult build-up before separation or divorce, coupled with the ordeal of leaving their child around the same time, the level of trauma you have suffered is likely to be high. There's no quick fix. Whatever your feelings for your ex, you need to grieve for the loss of your marriage. If you don't allow yourself enough time to feel and heal, you'll find yourself tripping over unfinished business. You have a lot to adjust to if you have recently separated from your child and your ex-partner so please treat yourself gently and allow yourself time.

LETTING GO

The first stage of letting go is accepting that what you had expected from the relationship and your ex was never going to be. What unrealistic expectations did you have? It's important to accept that your partner was never the generous, faithful, reliable (whatever fits) person that you hoped for when you first got together.

The second stage is acknowledging your unrealistic expectations and your role in the breakdown of the relationship. No matter how much you tried to control your ex you couldn't change him. You can see how your behaviour dovetailed his. I'm not talking about giving yourself a hard time. Simply acknowledge what was and is. You are likely to feel sad at this point. You're facing the loss of a dream or at the very least the reality of your relationship.

The third stage of the process of letting go is often made easier when it includes a physical manifestation of the process. Think of what is expressed at a funeral: a hearse driven slowly, dark clothing, carefully chosen readings, flowers for the grave, a coming together of family and friends to share grief and pay respects.

What ritual could you choose to help you let go of your past relationship? Writing the final letter of loss and release that you never send, the symbolic burning of old papers or letters, taking gifts that once held meaning for resale at a charity shop, throwing flowers into a river one a time, each one symbolising a facet of the relationship you are laying to rest.

Choose a ritual that has meaning for you and carry it out mindfully. Having a trusted friend witness your intent to let go can make the process more powerful. She or he will also be able to remind you of your commitment to let go and move on, particularly on days when life feels hard.

Having let go, with what are you going to fill the space you've created?

Nature fills a vacuum and before any negative aspects from the past have a chance to creep back in, now is the time to choose positive intentions for yourself and your future.

A really good starting point is your needs to-do list from the 'What's Yours is Mine' exercise above. In addition, ask yourself the following:

- What activities would boost your self-esteem?

- Do you want to revamp your living space or move somewhere else?

- How can you better nourish and affirm yourself?

- Is it time to learn a new skill?

- Does your work–life balance need your attention?

- Who or what do you need to commit yourself to?

- What are your first steps to make that incredibly indulgent, passionate or wacky dream happen in your life?

Take a deep breath. Let go. It's time for change.

Co-parenting and managing the difficulty of difference

Facing with courage the end of your relationship, understanding what went wrong and letting go of the past will mean that your continuing relationship with your ex, for the sake of your child, will be a lot less loaded. Big-hearted mothering—changing our attitude towards our capacity for loving and, as a result, sharing open heartedly our relationship with our child with her father—is a lot easier when you have reached a point of resolution and acceptance of the past.

That said, one of the biggest challenges facing all separated parents is reconciling differences on *how* to parent. If your child's home continues to run along the same or similar lines to when you were there permanently, you are lucky indeed (assuming that this philosophy was in line with your ideals and outlook).

Retention of the old order will probably be linked to the amount of hands-on parenting undertaken by your ex. However, a new wife might have at least an equal share in rearing your child and possibly even a greater proportion of it, especially if she has children of her own in their home. The less contact you have with your child, the less control you're likely to have over their upbringing and the greater the need for good communication skills and acceptance.

Who sets the upbringing ethos?

So just how much input and influence can you have when it comes to the way in which your child is brought up in their home?

Ideally discipline and routine that apply in his home and yours are most appropriately decided upon by both your ex-partner and you, but quite simply (which is not the same as *easily*), it boils down to how well you and your ex are able to communicate. We'll cover communication strategies in detail a little later.

Culture and atmosphere in the home your ex-partner has set up with someone else, on the other hand, has nothing to do with you. You'll have no say over the environment that your ex and his new partner create. That will be determined by their personalities and what they agree together. Ultimately, you have no direct control, unless of course you have serious concerns about your child's welfare and decide to approach the authorities or try through the courts system to change the status quo.

Assuming that your child's well-being is not seriously at risk, the reality is that your ex and his new partner have every right to decide upon their own lifestyle. And the more it differs from yours, the more likely it is that you'll have difficulty agreeing with it.

'It's the little things that get to me. His likes and dislikes when it comes to food, clothes, TV shows, things like that. I wonder how much of it is his father's influence and attitude and how much of it is down to his genes. I don't suppose I'll ever know but I do feel sad when I think of how different he is from me and how much he is like his father. Would he have been more like me if we'd had more time together before he became a teenager?'

Sharna

The first step towards accepting the upbringing ethos within your ex-partner's home is to let go of the old vision of your family. This is where the motto 'live and let live'

> IT'S WORTH REMEMBERING THAT
> DIFFERENCE IS NOT INFERIOR
> OR WRONG, EVEN THOUGH IT
> MIGHT SEEM LIKE IT TO YOU.
> IT'S JUST NOT THE WAY YOU
> CHOOSE TO LIVE YOUR LIFE.

comes into good use. Remember that as your children grow up they will make their own choices about how they want to live. They'll learn as much, if not more from experiences they don't like, so as long as the environment isn't abusive in any way, focus your attention and energy on living your *own* life instead of dwelling on theirs.

Be true to yourself and, by example, you'll show your children how to live honestly. Making lifestyle choices that are congruent with your own values and belief systems creates an important role model for your children. Living fully and taking responsibility for your actions carries a healthy and much more powerful message than spending time telling your child what's wrong with their dad's way of doing things.

LETTING GO EXERCISE

If you are having trouble letting go of how your family was in the past I suggest you try this exercise. As with the 'Reclaiming your Life' exercise above, choose a letting go ritual that symbolises the end of your family unit as it was living with your ex-partner.

It could be anything from replacing the dinner service you used as a family with one you choose by and for yourself to writing a letter you don't send, perhaps in the form of a declaration, starting for example as follows:

> *Letter to the world—on this day of …, I officially and energetically let go of my vision of my family unit as it was …*

When you've completed your letting go ritual, fill the space you've created with a new vision for your family.

Draw up a list of components that make up your own ethos of family and home life, creating your own traditions. Please try this exercise even if you don't have contact with your child. In doing so, you will be holding the space of 'your new family' which is important for both you and your child.

Just think, for once you don't have to negotiate! Include things that offer security, balance, light heartedness and fun—an ethos that represents *your* values and beliefs. It could include: 'No slamming of doors allowed', 'We will be honest with one another' or 'Saturday nights are chocolate night'. When you've written your new ethos list, pin it on the fridge door to remind yourself and others of the new order.

The importance of good communication

Talking to one another is something we do almost every day of our lives but we all know that an exchange of words from both parties doesn't mean that we're really hearing each other or saying the words that someone else is able to understand.

Please don't let any past experience of poor communication with your ex put you off. Instead of allowing yourself to despair over what has gone before, focus instead on creating the best communication channels possible between you and your ex. This might seem like a strange contradiction because as time passes his significance in your life will shrink, and yet you will almost certainly need contact with him over the years as you have a child together. Whether or not you like him, approve of his behaviour or even still love him, I urge you to work at developing the best lines of communication possible. If it helps, view it as the most important business relationship you'll ever have. Of course, we cannot make anyone speak or listen to us in exactly the way we would like them to, but we can learn to fine-tune the ways in which we communicate to invite a more positive response.

> *'Hindsight's a wonderful thing. I wish I had done more to communicate better with Trevor (ex-husband). I wanted to keep the peace, so I didn't really push for it. Having bipolar also meant that I lost confidence and spent so many years feeling guilty, like I didn't have the right to say anything and avoided discussions as a result. Perhaps it would have made a difference to Sami's upbringing and how things are between us now.'*

Danielle

(mother apart of twenty-two years)

We know that when guilt and negative feelings remain unchecked they debilitate us—we feel we don't have the right. Even the mother apart above, who has suffered hugely from the loss of her child as the result of bipolar disorder first experienced during postnatal depression, believes she could have done more. Maybe she could have—probably not.

But our long conversation, spanning over two decades of her being a mother apart, reinforced for me the importance of doing all that's possible to maintain reasonable communication with your ex.

Top tips: cornerstones of constructive communication

Be gracious. Why? Because you're strong enough to be and you'll feel better within yourself if you are. To act with grace means that you don't attack you ex, bring up his shortcomings or drag up the past. Stretching yourself to understand your ex's position and feelings—even if you don't agree with him—can go a long way to improving the relationship. There is nothing soft or unassertive about listening to him and feeding back your understanding. True listening often takes the force and sting out of an angry conversation.

Be aware and centre yourself. Before having contact with your ex, think yourself calm even if you don't have anything particular you want to say. Just being mindful of your inner strength, being healthily detached and aware of your boundaries will mean that you're on solid ground without even uttering a word.

Think creatively. When things feel stuck, try something else. Look for what you agree on as a starting point to build from. Appreciate your ex for what he does well—generosity engenders generosity. Try writing a letter when dealing with highly sensitive subjects. You can choose your words carefully, your ex will be less likely to misconstrue the written word and it allows time for reflection before a response. The story from the mother apart below shows what some creative thinking can achieve in what was a stalemate situation.

'For three years I tried asking my ex-husband to let me have access to my child and each time he told me that she didn't want to travel abroad to visit me. I never asked her directly as I didn't want to distress her. I suspected that it was him not her who was anxious about a visit. After talking it through with my therapist I decided to change my tactic. When I phoned my daughter I asked her whether she would like to fly over to see me. When she said she would, I asked to speak to her father. I told him that my daughter wanted to come. I suggested a date and assured him that she would be taken care of on the plane. I also asked him not to answer straight away, to think about it and I'd call again in week, and when I did, he agreed to the visit. Having a strategy, checking with my daughter directly and giving him time to think it through was a major breakthrough.'

Kathryn

Here is a strategy to ensure you keep tricky conversations on track.

W5H HOT ISSUE CONVERSATION PLAN

<u>What</u> **is the issue?** Be sure that you're as clear as possible in your understanding of the difficulty. You don't have to have all the answers but gather your thoughts, feelings and the facts.

<u>Why</u> **do you need to have the conversation?** Double check your motivation. Do you need to involve your ex or do you need to express your feelings with a trusted friend instead?

<u>When</u> **should you speak to him/them?** Don't knee-jerk into a response if you are upset or confused. Adopt the well known acronym of HALT—don't act if you're Hungry, Angry, Lonely or Tired. Calm yourself, reflect and plan. Timing is important. Ask your ex when a good time would be.

<u>Where</u> **will you talk?** Is a public space more neutral or will you feel more comfortable in your home or his?

<u>Who</u> **needs to be included?** Is the issue between you and your ex or does it involve his new partner too? Take great care before including your child in discussions. Most hot issue conversations should happen out of your child's earshot.

<u>How</u> **should you proceed?** A very useful model for having assertive conversations is the DESC (Describe, Express, Specify and Consequences) script designed by Sharon Bower in *Asserting Yourself: A Practical Guide for Positive Change.*

Describe the situation and/or your ex's action objectively. Include the time, place and frequency of the action without generalising or reacting emotionally to the behaviour. For example: 'When I've come to pick up Jenny for the last three weekends she hasn't been ready to leave. She says it's because you don't pick her up promptly after school on Fridays.'

Express how you feel with emotional restraint and without blame. Use 'I' statements as they are less defensive and provocative. Relate what you say to the goal to be achieved: 'I see her become stressed and rushed which is upsetting for me. I am also annoyed as we hit the rush hour traffic when we are late.'

Specify the outcome or behaviour you want. Be specific and only ask for one or two things at a time. If appropriate, say what you will change. 'Please supervise Jenny to pack her weekend bag the night before and pick her up promptly from school on Fridays. I could arrange to leave earlier and collect her from school if this is a problem for you at the moment.'

Consequences. Be explicit. Make positive consequences enough of a reward to maintain the behaviour and negative consequences that you're prepared to carry out and which 'fit the crime': 'Jenny will be less agitated and she won't have to listen to us sniping irritatedly at each other.'

FURTHER TECHNIQUES FOR CONFRONTING TROUBLESOME TOPICS

Prepare and practise what you want to say beforehand until it rolls off your tongue. Rehearse in front of a trusted friend and ask for feedback.

- Consider his likely reaction and formulate your response. Imagine the 'worst' thing he could say and how you could respond. Think assertion, dignity, self-respect and serenity.

- Come up with as many solutions or outcomes as possible—the more flexible you are, the more likely you are to get the result you want. This is not the same as caving in. Make sure you're clear about your fallback position, what's not acceptable to you.

- Don't rise to the bait, and be determined not to let things get out of hand.

- Say when you need time to think about his response

- If the discussion becomes heated, suggest that you both take time to think about it and talk again later.

In-laws or outlaws? Your child's relationship with your ex's family

For some mothers apart, the thought of their child being in the care of or influenced by their ex-partner's family feels like a bridge too far.

'I couldn't stand the man (husband's brother) when we were together and knowing that he's around my children drives me wild. My ex and his family think he's great fun, the

81

life and soul of a party, but he's arrogant, coarse, loud and immature. Because he plays with the children, they think he's great too but I worry that he's a bad influence.'

Helen

Just as with your child's father, she has a right to a relationship with her grandparents, aunts, uncles, cousins and other extended family. Instead of allowing yourself to react according to your feelings towards the in-law, start by asking yourself the following:

- Is there a reason why they shouldn't see your child?

- Are you concerned for her safety?

- Do you fear them trying to turn your child against you?

Dig deep for this one. Is there really a cause for concern or is it matter of personal difference?

If your ex-partner's family love your child they can provide things you can't—a different outlook on life, the perspective of a different generation. Extended families are important relationships and they should be encouraged and nurtured.

Tips for a truce and trouble-free co-parenting

- You can't change your ex. Each of you has chosen a path in life and it's important for you to move on and focus on what you have the power to change—opening your heart and being the best mother you can be to your children.

- It takes a long while to reframe a relationship. Don't give up. Keep learning from your mistakes.

- Avoid extremist thinking: begin to redefine frustrations with your ex as problems to be solved rather than as catastrophes.

- Choose your battles wisely. Ask yourself 'How important is it?' Accept that mistakes will be made by both of you. Reflect on whether you're somehow contributing to the problem between you and your ex and work on your contribution. Consider mediation if communication becomes very difficult between you.

🐾 Respect your child's relationship with your ex. It's completely separate from *your* relationship with your child. Remember that even though you might not like your ex, he is the person your child loves.

🐾 As a mother apart, open your heart to the reality that your children are on their own separate life path, living with their father. They will learn from their own experience.

🐾 We learn from difficulties and unhappiness—and that's true for your child too. It's not possible to protect our children from conflict nor does it help them in the long run.

🐾 Don't trouble yourself over the differences between your parenting style and your ex's. There are many ways of being a parent that support children to grow into happy, healthy adults.

Chapter 6

New wife … new mother?

'I was grateful that his new wife was providing a more constant mother figure for my children. But deep down I raged against her, this intruder into our lives.'

Vickie

A huge amount of energy goes into developing cooperative relationships after divorce and separation. And when step-parents are introduced into the equation, the challenge of co-parenting increases to include a third and fourth dimension.

Although most people understand the importance of striving for harmonious relationships in these circumstances, emotions are triggered easily when dealing with an exasperating ex, let alone his new wife. The real problem comes when we react from an unconscious emotional part of ourselves, or without thinking through the consequences of our actions or words. Old betrayals, anger, disappointments and unmet needs create a stony pathway set to trip us up rather than ensure what is best for children—or conciliatory and healing for us as we move on with our lives.

**If co-parenting and the introduction of an ex-partner's
new partner is hard work at the best of times, is it even a possibility
for mothers living apart from their children?
Yes, I believe it is.**

In this chapter we will examine the experience of co-mothering as a mother apart and explore the key to co-mothering without competition. We'll look at practical ways of creating the most productive co-mothering relationship possible before learning how to support your child to have a successful step relationship with the new wife.

A special note for those dealing with another kind of mother figure

For some mothers apart, a new mother figure comes in the shape of a mother-in-law, sister-in-law or other significant woman close to their ex-partner who fills the role of 'everyday mother' they once occupied. Sometimes they have been asked or invited to do so by the ex-partner and occasionally they step in as they perceive a need. The relationship that develops between your child and a new mother figure can be as significant and in some cases more influential than a stepmother, as one mother explains:

> '*My husband's mother has a strong influence on him—she is the family matri- arch. Apart from finding her overbearing at times, we got on okay but I wished that my husband didn't give in to her ways so much. When it was clear that our marriage was beyond repair, I moved out. I still can't believe how quickly she took over. She's there first thing in the morning to get the children ready for school. She drops them off and picks them up, looks after them and cooks for my ex before going home. I see her gaining more and more control. I'm sure my ex hasn't told her a lot of what we agreed concerning the children's upbringing, like discipline, watching TV, food and so on. I know from my ex that she blames me for the break-up. If she answers the phone when I call, the children are always 'out' or 'in the bath' and not able to speak to me. They were close to their Grandma while I was there and it hurts me to think that she has so much influence on them now. When I try to speak to my ex about it, he just shrugs his shoulders. I think it suits him this way.*'

Natalie

Although the focus of this chapter is on ex-partner's new wives, in no way do I underestimate the role and impact of a new mother figure, whoever she is, in your child's life. The feelings roused in you are likely to be much the same as towards a new stepmother and as such, you should find the ways of accepting and relating to her in this chapter appropriate and useful for you too.

What is the experience of co-parenting like for mothers living apart from their children?

Some mothers feel relieved at their ex-partner's new partner taking care of everyday practicalities. It's often the little things that niggle away at us, as remembering the detail is what many women, including the new wife, can be good at.

> *'Everything seemed to be more ordered and, dare I say it, calmer after Donna moved in. I used to worry about my children's physical care, whether they were eating enough fruit and veg, whether their clothes were washed and ironed, how often the bed linen was changed. My ex never bothered with the detail or forward thinking, like reminding the children to wear a coat when they went out. Knowing that another woman was living in my house wasn't easy, but in my case it did give me some reassurances.'*

Imogen

Others find the experience an extremely personal one and have an overriding sense of being substituted. It can feel threatening and be very distressing to think that another woman has taken your place in the family home—making changes to your child's routine, taking them to school, shaping and influencing them, comforting or encouraging them, treating them harshly or with indifference.

It can be particularly difficult if your ex starts a new relationship soon after yours has ended. Even if you're the one who left, divorce and separation is a painful business. It also means a lot of changes all at once—the loss of the relationship you once had hope for, a change to where you live, new plans for the future, what you can afford to do, how you spend your days and particularly how you pass your evenings. The end of the day is the time when mothers apart tend to feel the loss of their children most—the routine of doing homework, playing together, bath time, cooking the evening meal, sharing cuddles and hugs and a bedtime story.

Take heart, even though it might be painful, it *is feasible* to become more accepting of no longer having the level of everyday motherhood you once had.

It is possible to learn how to manage sharing your child with a new wife, and when necessary, play second fiddle to her too.

The key to co-mothering without competition

With the aim of finding peace of mind and personal happiness as your goal, the first step towards co-mothering is to practise lightening your outlook and opening your heart. This doesn't mean that we deny our loss or pain or any other feeling for that matter (as we know from earlier chapters, there are times when it's important to acknowledge and share painful and difficult feelings and take responsibility for them in our relationship with our child and others).

Instead we focus our energy on big-hearted mothering—developing our ability to sit with and manage our pain, to feel it without allowing our hurt to engulf and disable us, and expand our hearts to love more widely, beyond the narrow constraints of perceived ownership, expectation and rights.

As an alternative to trying to cling on and exert your status as biological mother or force others to recognise and respect your position as such, I suggest that you let go. By this I mean reducing the struggle and urgency inside you by centring on your potential for loving in a broader sense.

If we believe that we have to hold on tightly to others, even our children, then we squeeze and constrict the potential for that relationship. When we battle to control our connection with others, we find ourselves competing for recognition and love.

Your bond with your child will *always* be separate from anyone else's relationship with them—be it your ex-partner, his new wife, their grandmother. To think there isn't sufficient room for another woman to care for and maybe even grow to love your child is to misunderstand the nature and wonder of love. As Khalil Gibran, famous philosopher and poet, wrote so wisely and movingly in *The Prophet*:

> THERE IS NO COMPETITION. YOU ARE AND ALWAYS WILL BE YOUR CHILD'S MOTHER.

Your children are not your children.
They are the sons and daughters of Life's longing for itself.
They come through you but not from you,
And though they are with you yet they belong not to you.

There is nothing starry-eyed about this. As mothers apart, it's easy to hurt ourselves with thoughts of other mothers' intense attachments to their children. We agonise over how much closer we would be if only things had been different. We imagine that their father, his new partner or someone else is going to stake a claim on them, 'own' them more than we do, and use up the quota of love allocated to our child and ourselves.

If you believe there isn't enough love to go around, that your child isn't capable of loving both you and another mother figure, you will not only torment yourself unbearably but you could confuse your child, and make them feel guilty about feeling affection for someone else apart from you.

When we allow competitive feelings to take a grip and control us it causes us to feel jealous and fearful. Our world begins to shrink. We lose faith in ourselves, our worth and our loveableness. Our view of the life and what it has to offer us diminishes. Ultimately, we lose our peace of mind and, along with it, our ability to make ourselves happy.

The following story provides an example of big-hearted mothering that benefited a mother apart, her daughter and the stepmother.

> *'When I first heard my daughter call her stepmother "Mum" it felt like a knife turning inside me. Actually, she called me by my first name followed by Mum and the stepmother Mum. I was livid. Her stepmother should have been Tanya and I should be Mum, as that's what she'd grown up calling me until the divorce. As much as it hurt, I'm glad I said nothing about it at the time. I didn't want to back myself into a corner by insisting that I was the only Mum in her life. After thinking about things, including the fact that she was only five years old and that we wouldn't see each other that often, I decided that it was important to me that my daughter was happy and got along with her stepmother. If this meant that she had two mothers of equal status in name, then I would accept that even though it was hard for me. I made up my mind to see the benefits to my daughter of having two mothers—two differing points of view, two outlooks, two lots of love—rather than keeping the focus on my own feelings of rejection and upset. When times got tough, I told myself that I was her mother, that I loved her no matter what and that no one could take that away from me. My daughter is now an adult and she still has two mothers. She talks freely to me about her stepmother and I sometimes wonder if this would have possible if I had reacted badly to her arrival years ago. I'm glad I didn't. And I've been reinstated to Mum, which I'm a lot happier about.'*

Kathryn

It is possible to open your heart and love to the benefit and advantage of everyone, instead of reacting from a limiting belief system of scarcity. This mother apart has loved deeply over time. She acknowledged her feelings, as they were a normal reaction to the situation, but decided not to act on feelings of jealousy, pain or insist on her status as biological mother. As demonstrated by the now adult daughter's openness with her, she reaps the rewards of not having given in to her urge of wanting to possess her child. Trust and love have developed and she has drawn her daughter to her over the years. She has also provided an excellent role model to her daughter on how to love in a mature and respectful way.

How to co-mother from the inside out

A useful way to practise expanding our hearts to co-mothering without internal conflict is to challenge our individual fears about what we think we will lose by doing so, and replace these with more positive and healthy alternative thoughts.

Take some time to work through the exercises below to see what limits you and how you can support yourself to gain a more positive outlook.

Identifying love sapping beliefs

Our thoughts and assumptions shape our views on the world. They have a powerful effect on how we feel and in turn our feelings determine how we behave. It's important therefore to evaluate what we think because we have to accept a thought before it becomes a belief.

Fortunately it is possible to move beyond limiting beliefs. I hope you will have discovered this by doing 'The Out with the Fear' exercise in Chapter 2, in which you neutralised any fears you had about writing 'Your Story of Healing'.

The first thing you need to do is identify them. Make a list of the limiting beliefs you harbour about your child's relationship with their father's new partner or other mother figure by asking yourself: What fears do I have about losing out to a stepmother or mother figure in my child's life?

When writing your list, consider what you believe to be true about your role as a mother, exclusive relationships, your capacity to love, other people's ability to love you in return, the bond between mothers and their children and so on. Here are some examples.

> *'My daughter might forget about me'*
> *'My son could end up loving his stepmother more than he loves me'*
> *'My child might not know how much I love her'*
> *'I don't think my child is able to love two mothers—he's confused'*

Now that you know what you fear most about your child having a new mother figure, let's consider the antidote.

Building belief boost strategy

Reality check: Are you doing enough mothering? Take care when you ask yourself this question. This is not an opportunity to beat yourself up or go on a guilt trip. Quite simply, reality check each of the fears on your list to see whether there is anything else in your power that you could do to enrich the relationship with your child. Notice that I've written 'in your power'. If, for example, you are being denied contact, changing this at this moment is not going to be possible. On the other hand, deciding to phone your child every week, even though this is difficult or painful for you, or sending letters more often could deepen the bond between you.

Reality check: Are you doing too much? Are your fears at losing out to a stepmother or mother figure making you try too hard or hold on to your child too tightly? Release yourself from having to make up for not being the perfect mother. The reality is that *no one* is. Remember that having a full-time mother doesn't guarantee a loving relationship, greater stability or future happiness. I'm sure you won't find it too hard to think of a few examples of unhappy people who were brought up in what is considered to be a 'good' family. Many people who have estranged childhoods grow into well adjusted adults, find resolution for difficulties in their past where they need it and live meaningful, positive lives. Soften your urge to hold on tightly. Love your child deeply but gently. You *are* a good enough mother.

Action point: Choose and repeat affirmations that will support you. An affirmation can be a very powerful means of reprogramming the unconscious mind. Make them positive, short, in the present tense and in the first-person singular—for example, 'I am', 'I can'. Creating and saying affirmations out loud might feel odd or artificial to begin with but don't let this stop you. Repeat them regularly and in time negative beliefs will give way to a healthier, positive attitude. Some example affirmations are:

> *'I am completely open to giving and receiving love'*
> *'There is enough love to go round'*
> *'There is no competition—I am my child's mother come what may'*
> *'I send love unconditionally'*

Action point: Look after yourself. Treat yourself well. Take care of your health, make time to relax and ensure you have fun. Adopt an attitude that reinforces that you are your child's mother and that's a wonderful thing. Look at yourself in the mirror and tell yourself out loud that you are a good mother and there is no competition. Do this every day. Smile at yourself. Persist even if you feel uncomfortable. The more discomfort you feel, the more you need to practise.

**Even though it might seem difficult, without a doubt, the best way
forward is to try to develop a collaborative relationship with the new wife
or mother figure. This doesn't mean that you become friends but it does
mean you become friendly.**

You can succeed at non-competitive co-mothering because the only requirement is a change in *your* attitude towards the new wife or mother figure. Once again, it's your beliefs and mindset that determine what the world mirrors back to you. If you have a hostile attitude you're likely to attract a defensive response.

Now, I'm not suggesting that your partner's new wife will automatically respond warmly towards you if you make an effort to relate positively. What I do know is that there is definitely more chance of receiving the response you would like if you treat her cordially and with respect.

It's really very simple. Focus on the positive relationship you'd like to create instead of past hurts, frustrations or misunderstandings. It's simple because you're making a choice to prioritise your peace of mind and the well-being of your child. However, it's not always easy at first, and that's why it's important that you make a conscious effort to choose your attitude and the language to go with it.

Here are some more pointers to help you co-mother.

Think 'dignity'. Before every interaction with the new wife picture a dignified outcome. To make this happen, ensure that you conduct yourself in an honourable and self-respecting way. With a dignified relationship as a goal you can look beyond yourself and reach out to the dignity of your ex's new partner. Consider your choice of language. Watch your tone of voice. Even if she doesn't respond with grace to start with, don't give up. You will feel calmer and a greater sense of self-control from having related in a more considered and centred manner.

What is your body saying? Hold your body in a way that reflects your commitment to acting with dignity. Hold your head high and stand tall. Soften any tension or rigidity. Adopting a self-respecting posture will help you to connect to feeling this way about yourself. Smile before you meet the new wife. It might sound corny or fake but just try it. It will make you feel better about yourself, help remind you to let go of grudges and it might even get you a smile in return!

Keep things neutral. Keep topics of conversation light, uncomplicated and on common ground. Aim to be friendly. Even conversations about picking up times can be discussed courteously. There's no need to have anything more to do with each other than managing the care of your child, so keep it simple. With the pressure off, you might surprise yourself and discover a likeness or common interest.

Communicate clearly. We've already discussed the importance of clean, clear conversations when dealing with your ex-partner. Don't expect information to be communicated automatically from your ex to the new wife (and no, it won't happen by osmosis either). Treat her as an individual, respect her need to know and keep her informed. Check meanings when they are unclear and confront misunderstandings as soon as they occur.

Become interested in her as an individual. A good way to find out more about someone is to ask them for their views. Finding out about her approach or attitude towards something will mean that you'll have created the space to share yours. Asking her opinion will help to make her feel valued by you and, with a bit of luck, it should make her more inclined to consider your approach and outlook to parenting your child.

Appreciate her. Be willing to look for examples of the new wife's thoughtfulness, strengths and positive contribution. Welcome them and appreciate her. Everybody responds to compliments and thanks even if they find them hard to accept. That little, warm glow that you give her when you take the time to tell her that you appreciate her efforts could turn into the spark of goodwill—and, in time, a source of support when you need it most.

Don't take things personally. Watch that old chestnut guilt doesn't trigger you when you don't get the response you were expecting. If she didn't get back to you promptly or was offish at the door, avoid injuring yourself on the slippery slope of thinking that you've done something to upset her, that she doesn't like or approve of you, or anything else your inner critic might tell you. Other people, including the new wife, are busy, feel low, upset, challenged or distracted. Use your instincts. Ask for clarification when you need to, but don't automatically take it personally or imagine the worst.

Using these tips, try this exercise. Remember that reframing your attitude is within your control and adapting your behaviour can be a powerful force for change.

NEW WIFE RELATIONSHIP MAKE-OVER

Close your eyes and take a few slow, deep breaths. Relax. Now envisage the type of relationship you'd like to have with the new wife or mother figure. Imagine the way you would like to relate to her and see and hear her responding positively towards you. Visualise your collaboration improving over the years. With these thoughts in mind, write down your ideal co-mothering relationship.

Now think about the how things are between you at the moment. What could you change to strengthen the connection between you? Are there any differences that you need to discuss and find solutions to?

PLEASE SEE WORKING ON YOUR
RELATIONSHIP WITH THE
NEW WIFE AS A LONG-TERM
COMMITMENT. CHANGING YOUR
ATTITUDE IS RARELY SOMETHING
THAT HAPPENS OVERNIGHT. IT
TAKES COURAGE, PERSISTENCE
AND PATIENCE.

It might help to use the 'W5H Hot Issue Conversation Plan' for communicating with your ex in Chapter 5.

Expect to have to remind yourself regularly of your goal—to have the best relationship possible with the new wife, for your sake and that of your child and in time, perhaps, eventually for her sake too. With goodwill as your goal and the passing of time, you should begin feeling happier and more accepting of co-mothering your child.

Your child's life with the new wife

What to do when your child tells you they have a 'wicked stepmother'

If things are good between your child and the new wife, it's likely that accepting the value of this relationship in your child's life and allowing it to develop will be your biggest challenge. But what if they don't get along?

> *'When my son was eleven he came to stay for three weeks. It wasn't long before he started saying how much he disliked her stepmother, that she was too strict, she shouted at him, made him come home earlier than any of his friends and treated her own children a lot more leniently and fairly. He was very distressed and cried uncontrollably. I felt really upset. I couldn't bear to think that this woman was treating my son badly. I felt incredibly protective and hurt on my son's behalf. I felt guilty again. If I hadn't got ill, or had asked for help sooner, perhaps he would have still been with me and wouldn't be suffering like this now.'*

> *Danielle*

It can be extremely worrying to find out that your child isn't happy at home and the woman who is probably their primary carer doesn't seem to understand them or is treating them badly. It's possible for your feelings to be hooked and triggered by the past as much as, and sometimes more than, with your ex-partner. It's the stuff of fairytale nightmares. Our horror as little girls relived—reminded of the terrifying, evil stepmothers in Snow White, Hansel and Gretel, Cinderella and Vasalisa.

I grant you, it's not easy. As a mother apart, our child's conflict with their stepmother has the potential to spark off negative reactions on a number of levels—wicked stepmother fairy story mythology, a real life evil stepmother when we were growing up, neglect from our own mother, guilt and pain at not being a full-time mother, inadequacy at not being up to speed as a mother, not experiencing the learning curve of being a mother to a teenager and having to manage a crash course on it when a child comes to stay.

Be cautious. Take your time to sift though and reflect on what your child tells you. Remember that very few things in life need an instant decision or reaction.

Listen attentively to your child. Good listening will validate your child and give you a chance to truly hear and process what she says and doesn't say.

Work at keeping your feelings separate and be mindful of when your feelings are being hooked to past experiences. Read more about this in 'If your child complains about Dad' in Chapter 8.

Remember that you have the opportunity to help your child to learn how to communicate well and, once she has shared her feelings, help her to find a solution by asking similar questions to those suggested in Chapter 5: 'What could you say to (the stepmother) to explain your side and how you feel?' 'What do you think (the stepmother) is concerned or worried about in all this?' and so on.

Of course, if your child is very young or if the problem is a serious one you'll need to talk to your ex and the stepmother. Whether you talk to the new wife alone or with your ex-partner will be down to the nature of the problem and your knowledge of them as people. Agree a convenient time to talk and use the good communication guidelines in the previous chapter.

Supporting your child to have a successful step relationship

Your child's understanding of divorce, separation, living apart from you and the role of their stepmother will depend on their age and developmental stage. In Chapter 5 you will find a breakdown of typical changes and challenges facing your child which will help you know what to expect and adapt your behaviour to support her.

Just as your child has the right to his or her own relationship with their father, they will develop a relationship with their stepmother or mother figure, which is quite separate from you.

Enjoying the company of, seeing eye to eye with, learning from and indeed loving a stepmother is a child's right. If this feels hard, practise your affirmations to bolster your belief that there is enough love to go around. Take care of yourself and your feelings so that you can allow your child to love whomever they choose without feeling disloyal or guilty.

Here are some do's and don'ts to support your child's development for a healthy relationship with their new mother figure.

Don'ts

- Don't use your child as a confidant or emotional support. It's not your child's role to make you feel better or try to ease any competitive, threatened or jealous feelings you may have towards the new wife or mother figure.

- Just as with your child's father, don't speak badly of the new wife or their relationship to your child. Talk to trusted friends and practise letting little things go.

- Don't use your child as a messenger, the rearranger of visiting times or a bearer of instructions, letters or money.

- Don't set your child up as a spy to find out what the new wife gets up to or thinks.

- Don't be too hard on yourself. Having negative and painful feelings a normal, human response to a difficult situation. Remember, experiencing your feelings is different to acting on them. Let go of having to be perfect—sometimes it's enough just to bite your tongue when provoked and deal with your feelings out of earshot of your child or the new wife.

Do's

- Do have an open attitude so that your child feels free to talk about the new wife. The more accepting and easygoing your attitude the more relaxed your child will be and, with practice, you will be too.

- Do let your child know that you are glad when they are happy and have a good time, even when this involves the new wife.

🔖 Do try to look for and acknowledge to your child any of the new wife's personal strengths, good points and advantages, of having her in their life.

🔖 Do try to welcome difference with your child. The manner and attitude of a new wife can form an excellent basis for broadening their outlook or, at the very least, learning about tolerance and diversity.

🔖 Do remember to value yourself. This means nurturing yourself on days when you find big-hearted mothering tough. It also means appreciating yourself when you make a special effort to the benefit your child or build on your relationship with the new wife. Valuing yourself is also to lighten up, ease off and see the funny side wherever possible. There's nothing like a good laugh to help relieve stress and gain perspective—and as a mother apart, there'll always be surreal or bizarre times to find the humour in.

Chapter 7

In love vs. mother love: how to have the relationship you deserve and be a mother apart

Contrary to the stereotype of the selfish, abandoning mother who runs off to please her own desires without a twinge of remorse, the reality for many of us is very different. Whether or not another partner is in the picture at the time of separation, all too often mothers apart embark on new relationships too heavy with the burden of sorrow and guilt, and too light on self-acceptance, self-esteem and self-love.

Perhaps you long for a loving relationship, an opportunity to put the past behind you and find fulfilment and commitment with someone special. Maybe you feel too hurt, damaged or burned out from previous bad experiences and swear that you'll never make yourself that vulnerable again. Or you might believe that if a relationship happens, it happens.

**Whatever you feel about love and whether you have a partner or not,
you deserve a good relationship.**

I believe that relationships have the capacity to bring us home to ourselves. They challenge us to go beyond what we think we can give and receive. With a commitment to honesty, learning from love and our part in the union—even though this is scary and difficult at times—a loving relationship can provide us with the intimacy, support and growthfulness that we long for.

This chapter will guide you through some key points to help you assess your readiness and your hopes, needs and fears for a new relationship. We'll consider some remedies for some typical mothers apart relationship flashpoints as well as exploring whether having another child is the right decision for you.

We'll start from a place of self-love and nurturance.

Are you ready for a new relationship?

After you've read each of the questions below, close your eyes and reflect on your response. Be as honest as possible. If you are unsure of your readiness, try turning the question into a journaling exercise. Taking the fourth question as an example, turn it into a heading: 'Why do I want a new relationship?' and write freely, exploring your feelings to answer it.

Are you on the rebound? It's said that dating soon after a break-up is fine as long as you don't take it too seriously or get yourself heavily involved. I understand that the desire to go out with someone new or maybe even someone who's been in the wings for a while can feel irresistible, especially if you've been unhappy, lonely and it's been years since you've experienced the excitement of exploring possibilities with someone different. But I urge you to be cautious and take good care of your heart if you are newly separated. As a mother apart you've lost a lot, perhaps a marriage and a child. Try to resist the urgency itch. Give yourself some time out to reflect and just be.

Have you let go of your last relationship and dealt with emotional issues? You may desperately want things to be different this time but unless you understand the dynamics of your last relationship and your part in it—and have truly let go of your ex—you're likely to trip up over the past. If you were treated badly or betrayed it will take time before you'll be able to restore your faith and trust again. If you had a parent who abused you, you're likely to attract partners who continue this pattern of abuse. The more conscious you are of your patterns of attraction (and we all have them), the more you'll be able to nose out and walk on by unhealthy connections. If you're having difficulty resolving issues, please find a therapist to help you.

How do you feel about yourself? In order to distinguish when you're receiving healthy love and attention from another you need to believe in your own worthiness, to honour yourself. It starts with you—you set the standard. Feeling guilty and worn out by pain, mothers apart are prime candidates for corrosive self-beliefs which can lead to self-loathing and low self-worth. Please take time on your own to get to know yourself again. Are you aware of your value and uniqueness—your strengths, gifts and abilities? Start or return to self-affirming activities and hobbies, whether it be knitting or African drumming. Make sure you have some fun. Give something back to the world too. Being of service to others and offering small acts of kindness to those around you can really boost your confidence. It is genuine love and respect for yourself that will guide you to make good choices.

Why do you want a relationship? Don't dismiss this question as being obvious; instead be really honest with yourself. Does the loss of your child feel so great that you feel you need to fill the empty space inside? Are you looking to recreate a family to make yourself 'respectable' and contact with your child easier? Do you hope that a new partner will act as a buffer or defence against your ex, his family or the system? Reasons like these are unrealistic, unfair and potentially damaging to yourself and a would-be new partner. While a new partner can help you, the unique challenges of being a mother apart are yours to face, heal and learn from. There are many good reasons for wanting a relationship but the happier, more fulfilled and able you are to love yourself and take care of your own needs, the greater your chances of relationship success.

Are you able and willing to commit to and work at a new relationship? Search your soul. Is this really the right time in your life for a new relationship? Do you have the capacity right now? Knowing your limits is a strength. Relationships bring joy but they also bring conflict; it's the nature of love. Have you got enough emotional energy to give to your new partner, get to grips with being a part-time Mum, process your feelings, move house and … (you fill in the blank) all at the same time? Perhaps yes, perhaps no. Remember that 'not right now' doesn't mean never and if there's a deep connection and honesty between you and someone else, moving on with the relationship can wait.

Fantasy and reality and the nature of love

There is so much I would like to say about the nature of love in intimate, sexual relationships. The temptation to write more is great, especially as I know that mothers apart have an extraordinary capacity for loving and letting go, remaining open and holding on. Just as I've encouraged you to face the reality of life apart from your child, to uncover the roots of your guilt and pain, I urge you seek out and strive for reality in your partnership with a mate. It's reality—facing what is with honesty, openness and willingness—that nourishes love and creates greater intimacy, not keeping the peace or keeping things happy.

But writing about love in sexual relationships isn't the topic of this book and so I refer you to the book of a wise woman—my teacher and supporter Anne Geraghty. In her book *How Loving Relationships Work: Understanding Love's Living Force*, Anne writes with great knowledge and understanding on how love works and what it needs. She explains that there are many ways of falling in love and how it happens will influence your relationship, that our primary struggle is often not with our partners but with the demands and responsibilities of love, that it's instinct not knowledge that reveals the way of love, and that there is always an equality in a relationship although this is often hidden.

If you would like to learn more about deep intimate love and learning, I leave you in Anne's capable hands.

Moving on, mulling over and moving in

Okay, so you know you're ready. You've met your new love and you're considering increasing your commitment to each other. The reality is that you're going to need really good communication skills if you're going to have enough capacity to live a meaningful life together as a mother apart, as a step-parent, with your child, perhaps his child and maybe even a child together.

Try the exercise below, preferably before you start living together. Although you might fear your partner's response to what you say or what he or she might reveal to you, be as honest as possible—after all, this is a big investment of love and life for both of you.

NEEDS, HOPES AND FEARS EXERCISE

Your goal is to understand more about one another's hopes, fears and experiences. This is both an exercise in communication as well as a valuable source of information about each other. Observe the subtle things your partner says and doesn't say that they might not even be aware of—the silences, facial expressions, gestures.

Agree a time to talk when no one else is around. Take turns to describe to each other what you feel a loving relationship should look like. What is important to each of you? What makes you feel loved, understood and cared for? What makes you feel neglected, taken for granted, fearful? When you talk about the past, don't talk about ex-partners. Make it detailed—nothing is too trivial. Don't interrupt each other. Just listen. When you have both had a turn, don't enter into discussions about what was said right away. Observe the differences and similarities and allow some time, perhaps even a few days, for your views to filter before discussing each of your experiences.

Try this process again to explore your hopes and fears on becoming a stepfamily.

There are as many reasons why relationships end as there are people facing this difficult decision in their lives. Even when an ending is fairly amicable there is still sense of loss and perhaps even guilt as both parties ask themselves whether they tried hard enough, whether meeting their need to leave was justified or worth it and so on. There is, however, one reason for leaving that tends to make mothers apart particularly vulnerable to the judgement of others as well as trigger what can be a strong guilt reaction within themselves.

IF YOU LEFT TO BE WITH A LOVER

'I couldn't cope with the guilt at having the affair and told my husband about it within a few weeks. We'd been together for seventeen years and we'd slowly drifted apart. We

have different interests in life—he didn't see that. He was gutted when I said there was no chance of working things out between us. There was never any question in my mind that our son should stay with him. He wasn't the guilty party and I didn't want to disrupt my son's life. My son was very hurt and blamed me and refused to see me. He told me in no uncertain terms what a bad mother I was. It only lasted six months between me and the other man. That was two years ago and my son is still hostile towards me.'

Alex

'Coming out as a lesbian at the same time as admitting I was unfaithful made it even harder. I wanted joint custody and I didn't want this to go against me in court. When I talked about a divorce he became very upset and pleaded with me not to take the children away from him. I felt guilty and worn down from being a mother, that's why I agreed they could stay with him. I didn't want to unsettle the children. I had so much to deal with—we all had a lot to cope with. I feel really bad about everything happening at once and what the children have had to come to terms with.'

Sonia

If your circumstances are a version of leaving for a lover, you may be especially susceptible to feeling guilty—and this means that you're going to have to work extra hard to move on from this mindset in order to give yourself, your partner and your child a future of peace and happiness.

Try this exercise. Sit on a chair and put another chair in front of you. Project any negative feelings and judgements onto this chair—imagine pulling together all the things you say to yourself and others have said to you and sending them to sit outside of yourself. For example, your bundle of negativity might contain a pile of guilt, a ball of shame, that spiteful thing your ex-partner said to you when you left, the awful thing your child called you on the phone, the vicious things you say to yourself about being such a bad mother and so on.

Now read the following message from me to you:

Dear …

Please stop giving yourself such a hard time. Although I don't know the details of your situation I do know that it takes two people to make a relationship. What was going on under the surface layer of your relationship? What truths did you both ignore?

Perhaps there was a better way than having an affair to express and deal with the difficulties you experienced. Maybe there wasn't. Either way you serve no one by keeping negative feelings, beliefs and judgements alive within you. Each time you chastise or blame yourself you pick away and reinfect a wound that more than anything else needs time alone to heal. Feeling bad about yourself won't improve your relationship with your child or nurture your new relationship. More importantly, it will poison your love for and belief in yourself.

Please stop treating yourself badly about what you did or didn't do and don't allow others to put you down. Quietly protect yourself. If you need to make amends to someone, do so. After that, turn your attention to the future. Put your energy into your relationships with the people you love. Remember, love is never wasted even if all you are able to do is send love from afar—you never know what the future holds.

Go well.

Now see if there is anything you would like to tell your bundle of guilt and judgement. Think of what you could say to silence the messages and loosen its control over you. For example: 'I am not a (whatever it is you've been called or think of yourself as)', 'I deserve love and happiness', I do not have to suffer forever for my actions', 'I did the best that I could at that time'.

Finally, close your eyes and imagine yourself picking up the bundle of negativity and guilt and disposing of it. Visualise yourself at a cliff's edge, throwing the bundle into the sea below or into a big, crackling fire and watching it go up in flames. Or perhaps digging a hole in a far-off field and burying it to be organically broken down and recycled. Choose what has meaning for you. Let it go. If you sense yourself feeling bad or reliving the past with should's and could's, stop. Take yourself back to your disposal site and dump the damaging thoughts and messages with renewed intent.

Although this process might seem simple, it can be very powerful. Whatever happened, please motivate yourself to move on from the bad feelings associated with leaving for someone else. They are of no use to anyone.

First aid for flashpoints: mothering apart and new relationships

Let's troubleshoot some common new relationship complexities.

'MY PARTNER JUST DOESN'T UNDERSTAND EVEN THOUGH HE/SHE TRIES HARD!'

As close as you are to your partner, as much as you love each other, the reality is that he or she isn't a mother apart and will never understand exactly how you feel. Just because your partner doesn't share your experiences doesn't mean that you're incompatible. That said 'he/she tries hard' is a good start as it shows commitment and willingness. How you communicate is key. It's your responsibility to tell him/her how you feel and what you need. Help them to understand. Asking for support isn't enough. What does support mean to you? Be as specific as possible. Do you want to him/her to sit and listen, give you a back rub, cook the dinner or help you come up with a creative solution?

> ALLOWING YOUR PARTNER TO SLIP INTO THE ROLE OF YOUR COUNSELLOR WILL PUT A STRAIN ON YOUR RELATIONSHIP. YOU WILL CEASE TO BE EQUAL PARTNERS AND WILL UPSET THE BALANCE OF POWER AND VULNERABILITY BETWEEN YOU.

If you are experiencing a lot of pain, confusion, anxiety or other strong feelings, please find additional support from someone outside your relationship—a friend, counsellor or organisation such as MATCH.

'I FEEL TORN BETWEEN MY CHILD AND MY NEW PARTNER'

Time with our children is special. We want to give our all, our full attention, to catch up, give hugs, have chats, do fun things. We also want to feel connected and spend adult time with our partner and before long we feel exhausted, torn between the two. What can be done? First of all, relax. Being pulled in different directions will make you feel overstretched and tense. To feel that you can't relax is a sign that you need to, as a matter of urgency. Tell your partner that you feel torn and check their experience. Perhaps he or she isn't expecting as much attention from you when your child comes to stay and you are putting unnecessary pressure on yourself.

Structure and manage your time well. Decide and agree one-to-one time with your child, family time and time alone with your partner. Planning and agreed understanding will take away a lot of pressure. When you schedule adult time, make sure it's pleasurable for both of you. Ask for his help to make that time longer and easier—for example, having the washing up done and the DVD in the player by the time you finish the bedtime story.

You can manage the expectations of your child too. Having boundaries help your child feel safe and contained. Saying a loving goodnight after a great day out—explaining that it's now time for Mum and Jeremy to have time together—is good for all of you.

If you're feeling very torn, do a reality check. Are you trying to avoid feeling guilty by giving too much? Stop and revisit Chapter 2. Are you trying to be Supermother? Reread and implement the self-care techniques in Chapter 4.

'I'M SO ENVIOUS—MY PARTNER HAS REGULAR CONTACT WITH HIS/HER CHILDREN'

Step-parenting is challenging for everyone but to find that you spend more time with your partner's children than your own can feel like a cruel twist of fate if you're a mother apart. Acknowledging your envy is a start. Without the expectation that your partner can change your circumstances, sharing feelings of jealousy and loss will make him or her more aware and hopefully responsive to your sensibilities. Be mindful of your tolerance and resentment levels and set your personal boundaries accordingly. Don't make your partner or the children, who have no control over their circumstances, slave to your emotions. But it will be less painful if conflict, discipline and respect issues are dealt with quickly and constructively.

Allow your partner time alone with his or her children. It's important for them and, more significantly, it will allow time for you to take care of yourself. Don't do the house-work if they have a day out together—make sure you use it as 'me time'. Pamper, soothe, stimulate, invigorate—do whatever you fancy, whatever you need. If you are a stepmum without contact with your own children you'll need a first-class self-care routine.

Don't try to replace your partner's children's mother. They already have one and you might be more vulnerable than you realise—needy for love from a child—than is reasonable in a step-parent/stepchild relationship. Instead, try to complement their mother's role in the capacity of a good friend.

'I FEEL GUILTY ABOUT FEELING HAPPY WITH MY NEW PARTNER'

How much does guilt affect your new relationship? Are happy days and light-hearted moments undermined by an invasive inner critic telling you that you aren't worthy? If guilt is a problem to you and you haven't worked through the exercises in Chapters 1 to 4, I encourage you to do so. Guilt distorts reality. It also sucks the lifeblood out of pleasure and joy. You deserve happiness and love that is based in reality. If guilt is holding you back, please consider working with a counsellor to find resolution.

It is important to honour and prioritise time with your partner that is kept separate from family time. Difficulties, conflict and issues that are part and parcel of being a mother apart and step-parent are not sexy. Spending too long focusing on family issues instead of making love will take its toll on your relationship. Make your bedroom an uncluttered, relaxing sanctuary that both you and your partner enjoy retiring to. Keep it an adult space for you and your partner only. The love you express between you forms the bedrock of your family. Your child and your partner *need* you to be happy. Please do all that you need to make sure that you are.

Having a child together

Having a child in a second relationship is a big decision for couples in stepfamilies where contact with children from previous relationships isn't an issue. For mothers apart the emotional stakes are high. Having another child for the wrong reasons or at the wrong time can cause heartache and reopen wounds. That said, choosing to have a baby for the right reasons in a new, loving relationship can be fulfilling and wonderful for you, your partner and the child you live apart from.

The decision-making process should consider your well-being and that of the baby, your partner, your child, any children that your partner has and anyone else either of you has responsibility for. That's lot of people to take into account. In weighing up the pros and cons, having a narrow focus of just the two of you could throw up some unexpected hardships later on.

The questions below will help you decide whether or not to have another child.

- Are you trying to fill the space left by the child you live apart from? No matter how many children you have, none of them can replace the one you live without. Please take care. The physical and emotional impact of having a new baby has the potential to bring up memories and act as a trigger for loss and grief.

- Do you feel empty or lonely?

- Are you stuck in the grief cycle described in Chapter 3?

- Do you feel like you're missing part of yourself?

🐾 Are you ignoring or minimising your own needs? We know that to the outside world mothers apart appear to put their own needs above those of others. However, a common theme in our lives is to allow our feelings of guilt to make us over-responsible and give more than we're comfortable with giving, and it allows our shame to make us believe we deserve less than others.

🐾 Are feelings of low self-worth making you ignore or minimise your need for personal fulfilment, financial security, time to heal after a painful divorce or enough time to really get to know and trust your partner before having another baby?

🐾 Can you think of other ways you might be abandoning or neglecting yourself?

🐾 Who wants a baby—you or your partner? If it's your partner, are you confident of his or her motives for wanting a child? Is there a chance that he or she is trying to fill a gap or is ignoring the need to heal his or her own pain or loss? Exploring how and who broached the subject of having a child can throw light on the motivation behind the idea and give you some good clues about whether or not it's a good idea.

🐾 Is this the right time for you? A sense of urgency about whether you should or shouldn't have a child might indicate you're not grounding your decision-making process in reality. If you know you have a tendency to rush into things, slow down. Tell yourself that babies are too important to be hurried.

🐾 If you feel pressure to have a baby soon, what do you think is behind your sense of urgency? What do your instincts tell you? Even if you're satisfied that your reasons for having a baby are realistic it's a good idea to double check at a deeper level. When you're alone, close your eyes and listen carefully to the message of the wise woman within you.

🐾 Are you in tune with your instincts about your readiness and that of your partner? Should you wait a while longer? You don't have to give a reason why—just feeling or sensing you should wait is valid reason enough.

🐾 Do you really long for a child or are your instincts telling you that you really need to be giving birth to something else—perhaps a creative project, a business venture or yourself through a therapeutic process?

Having satisfied yourself that wanting another child feels right for you, why not try the following exercise with your partner?

POSITIVELY PREGNANT PLEDGES

There are fewer feelings more joyful than being pregnant when you truly, deeply want to be. Write a list of all the positive reasons you can come up with for having a child. Ask your partner to do the same and talk about the similarities and differences.

Some of your reasons could include:

- I want to share one of life's most joyous and challenging experiences with the person I love.

- Having a baby is the fruition of our relationship. It's the right time; the baby will be conceived in an atmosphere of love and peacefulness.

- Now that my divorce is finalised and I have had time to heal, I'm ready to have the child that both of us long for.

Some points to ponder as you develop your new relationship

- Stepfamilies are a reorganisation of biological families. They function differently and are not created instantly.

- The presence and impact of absent children is greater than you think. Managing life with children who visit occasionally is almost always more difficult than life with children who live with you.

- It is natural for you to feel more committed to your own child, even though your aim is to treat children in the family equally.

- Children do not always get on well with their step-parent even if they treat that child extremely well.

- Focus on building relationships one day at a time. Be patient, this is the work of your lifetime.

- Be prepared for surprise and change—anything could happen at any time.

Chapter 8

Changes and challenges: helping your child cope with divorce and separation

Nothing is permanent. The only thing we can really be sure of is change. Some changes are harder to cope with than others, and it's our attitude to managing loss and how we learn from our experiences that determines our growth and serenity.

You can't avoid loss—it is part of life. As great as our instinct might be to protect our child, to cushion the blows, the painful reality is that the sooner we as mothers and they as children learn this unavoidable truth and begin accept it, the less we will suffer. But just how much do children suffer when parents separate?

The impact of divorce and separation on a child

Rest assured that most the recent research on the effects of divorce and separation on children show that although children experience emotional, social and cognitive upsets during the initial 'crisis' phase , after a year or so, most children move into the 'adjustment' stage after losing a parent or as a result of remarriage of a parent. After two years, a marked improvement was noted. Follow-up after six years showed that children from divorced families were more independent than their peers, tended to grow up quicker and have increased decision-making skills. Research also shows that conflict within a marriage, particularly before divorce, needs to be taken into account as much as the effects of separation itself.

A recent report published by the Joseph Rowntree Foundation stated that at least one in three children will experience their parents separating before the age of sixteen, so the experience of her family splitting up won't feel that unusual for your child. It also reported that while many children go through a period of unhappiness, children are usually helped by good communication with parents and most settle back into a normal pattern of development and finding ways to help your child with this is the focus of this chapter. We will start with support for changes and challenges that your child might experience before moving on to strategies to help both your child and you manage her anxiety, anger and her relationship with her father during times of difficulty.

Helping your child with changes and challenges

Children react to divorce and separation according to their individual character and the circumstances of the family break-up. One child might act out in anger and another might withdraw.

Your job is to watch carefully and monitor your child the best way you can—in other words, *in ways that are within your power*. This includes helping your child find strategies for dealing with their pain and loss. In so doing, you will be supporting your child to find the tools to manage the many losses she will experience in her life.

Depending on your situation this could mean observation on a regular or irregular basis, when you see her, and asking for information from others to gain a full picture of her behaviour. If you are denied contact, your work will be to take extremely good care of *your* well-being, and to try as much as is wise for you, either in person or via a third party, to check your child's progress.

Please use what's written below as a guide not as a guilt trip. My aim is to inform you of what might come up and reduce the surprise factor to help you move more easily into supporting your child and dealing with your feelings. It's important to bear in mind that the changes and challenges listed are not exclusive to children who live apart from their mother. They are what is commonly regarded as possible behaviours and beliefs of children who experience their parents divorcing or separating. Please remember: your aim is to be a good enough parent, doing the best you can—not a perfect parent.

Tell her it's not her fault. Being so obvious, this fact might get overlooked and yet children of all ages can believe that their parents have separated because of something they have done. Even if your child doesn't verbalise any self-blame, assure her that your separation is an adult decision made by you and her father. Whatever her age, tell her repeatedly that she has not caused your divorce or separation. Give your child books that explain divorce and separation appropriate to her age and read them to her where possible. You will find a list of suggested reading in the Bibliography.

Be truthful. Be as honest as possible with your child. Tell her you are not abandoning or rejecting her. Sometimes young children think that because parents stop loving each other they might stop loving them. Assure your child that you will always love her even though the feelings between you and her father have changed. Tell her that you and her father will continue to take care of her (if this is true), even though you won't be living together, spelling out how this will happen in practice. Where possible let your child know how often and where you will see her, and how it will change her life on a daily basis. Do the same for grandparents and other family and friends whose point of contact is through you.

The fantasy of reconciliation. Children of all ages can hold on to hope that their parents will get back together again. This is normal and you can help your child by telling her that it is usual for children to want this, but this is not going to happen—your separation from her father is permanent.

Black and white thinking. Try not to be too alarmed if your child takes sides or holds judgements about marriage, believing that you or her father have broken the rules. The frequency of divorce will mean that her peers are likely to experience separation too, which will help her to feel less alone. You can help as well by modelling behaviour that is free from criticism or blame of her father.

Growing up too quickly. Teenagers of divorced parents can feel more mature than their peers and might assume greater responsibility for their younger siblings or concern themselves with finances and other adult worries. Your child might take on more than they can cope with peers or mix with older friends. Please don't panic and remember that there are many reasons other than divorce that could trigger this kind of behaviour in teenagers. Do your best to stay in touch and keep the lines of communication open. The next section will help with this. Listen to your child and maintain an interest in her hobbies. Encourage and appreciate her talents, intelligence, her opinions and intuition. Reassure yourself that it is normal for teenagers to think and talk about leaving home as they are reaching the stage when they can make such decisions.

Guidance for times of difficulty

This section is designed to guide you should you ever be in the position of supporting your child through difficult times. Once again, please remember to keep things in perspective as you read—the worry, anger, struggles and challenging behaviour discussed are not the preserve of the child who lives apart from her mother. Children can experience difficult emotions for a variety of reasons, whether they live with both parents or one.

If your child becomes worried or anxious

Let's start with a reality check—worry and anxiety is part of what we experience as people. Living apart from you, your child is likely to struggle with these feelings to a lesser or greater degree. They might also show physical symptoms of anxiety, such as headaches, tummy aches, nausea, diarrhoea as well as bed-wetting and thumb sucking if she is very young. It's important to note that children, particularly when very young, might regress in their behaviour and slip back from their latest development milestone.

Rest assured that in time regressed behaviour should disappear and normal development will return.

What should you do if your child becomes worried or anxious? First of all, share *your* feelings of worry with someone you trust. Take care of yourself you wouldn't want to add to your child's anxiety or set up an unhealthy pattern of your child taking care of your feelings.

Try to encourage your child to talk about any fears she might have and when she does, listen well. Listening and giving someone your full attention without jumping in too soon with your answer or feedback, validates them it also builds trust.

> **By truly listening, you convey to your child that her feelings, experiences and views are legitimate and significant—that they are important and they matter.**

Be sure to listen for what isn't being said too. Watch her body language as this will help you to get a full picture of how things are.

As much as you would like to, you can't fix your child's feelings but you can reassure your child by reflecting back what she says and asking open questions. Open questions are usually invitations to consider, starting with how, what and where, that can't be answered with a 'yes' or a 'no'. For example:

> *'I can see that you're worried about …'*
> *'Maybe you're not feeling loveable because I don't get to see you very often …'*
> *'I can hear that you're upset …'*
> *'What can I do to help?'*

By listening actively you will let your child know that you understand and care, and can offer comfort. Even if it's not within your power to give your child precisely what she wants or needs, listening to and understanding her anxieties will give you information to change what you can. Sometimes little changes make a big difference.

Respond to your child honestly. It is much better to say you don't know exactly when you'll see her again than to try to save her and you from your feelings.

Be prepared to hear and respond to the same fear several times. Repeating her worry and hearing your response and

REASSURE YOUR CHILD THAT THEY ARE LOVEABLE AND THAT YOU WILL ALWAYS LOVE THEM— AGAIN AND AGAIN. VERY SMALL CHILDREN DON'T UNDERSTAND THE CONCEPT OF 'ALWAYS' SO REPEATED REASSURANCE OF YOUR LOVE IS ESSENTIAL.

reassurance will be part of her process of understanding and coming to terms with how her life has changed.

THE NEED TO REVISIT AND RESPOND OVER THE YEARS

'My boys needed to go over what happened, why we lived apart regularly through their childhood. When they spent time with me, we developed this little custom of looking at the old photo albums together—their father and I when we married, their birth, life together as a family—and they would ask what happened and why we separated. They asked different versions of the same questions over and over. I watched how they understood more as they got older. They asked more questions as they got older as well.'

Patti

This mother was able to give her children the information they needed appropriate to their age through their photo album ritual which provided a good prompt and a quiet, reflective time for questions. Your child's capacity for understanding the past will change as she grows older.

Be willing to answer questions repeatedly over the years, as this will be one of the ways your child will come to terms with the separation.

Think of ways that you can give your child 'permission' to ask. Old photos are a great idea but just talking about the past will demonstrate that you're open to discussion. For example, 'Do you remember the garden in our house in Watling Street?', 'Can you remember Sally dancing at Uncle John's wedding?' and the like can make good openers.

If your child becomes angry

Be assured that feeling angry is an appropriate, normal and healthy response. It's the destructive expression of anger that is of concern. Repressed anger can result in depression, so if you are in a position to do so, watch out for changes in sleep patterns, appetite, lack of interest in friends and usual activities. Take any mention of suicide seriously and get professional help immediately. Other destructive expressions of anger can include substance abuse and delinquent behaviour. Remember, feeling angry isn't the problem but what we do with it can be. If you are in a position to, guide your child to express any anger they might feel in a healthy way, which doesn't include hurting anyone else.

Once again, reflect on how *you* express anger and how *you* feel about anger in others. If this is a difficulty for you, please find the help you need to understand and process your feelings.

Encourage your child to talk about their feelings even though it's sometimes tough to hear. I understand how painful it is for mothers apart to hear the angry things their children throw at them, so here are some strategies to guide you.

RECEIVING YOUR CHILD'S ANGER

'Sometimes we have an exchange of text messages because she won't talk to me directly, and she writes such hurtful things and I can't believe how angry she is at what's happened. It is bad enough when it's about things that I caused but she blames me for the hard times she had at the hands of (her father and stepmother) as well.'

Olivia

It takes big-hearted mothering to withstand the force of your child's anger. I encourage you to be willing to hear your child say that she is angry with you. I urge you to listen without justifying your actions should your child ever say that you are the cause of all her problems, you've ruined her life, she hates you.

Although I understand that this is really hard, I encourage you to be strong. Try to regard the fact that your child is expressing herself to you, even though it's nothing but blame and anger right now, as a positive thing. Why? Firstly, she's connecting with you. Secondly, she feels safe enough to show her anger.

As difficult as it might be, please see your child's expression of anger as her process—the stuff she has to deal with—and not see it as punishment.

Should it come, just hear it. A torrent of rage is not the time to try to fix or change anything. Know that you probably won't be able to say the 'right' thing. Your child won't let you say the 'right' thing. She's not ready to let go of the past and move on right now. Right now, nothing will be right for her.

Some mothers apart face expressions of rage as their child grows up and others can experience it out of the blue from an adult child.

'For some reason my daughter hates me. She didn't invite me to her graduation, although I attended. I was so pleased when all four of my children were at my fiftieth birthday party but she was only out to cause trouble. I think she accepts my gifts but badmouths and ignores me. WHY? I may never know. I feel hurt, rejected—she is her father's

116

daughter in that respect—but I thought her being a daughter who witnessed a lot of what went on (domestic violence) would understand! I was wrong.'

Melanie

The important thing is to find a way to let your child express her anger without letting the content of what she says affect you too much. If you experience an angry outburst, take some time to centre yourself. Remind yourself of your 'Trusted Friend Reality Check' in Chapter 2. Hold this within you: you did the best you could at the time of separation. Then listen to your child and acknowledge her pain—say something along the lines of:

'I know you are very angry …'
'I wish I knew what to say to help …'
'I'm truly sorry that things have turned out this way …'

Whatever feels real and right. And don't allow yourself to believe any negative inner messages along the lines of being 'the worst, most despicable mother in the world'. There is no need to as you are *not*—and being hard on yourself won't serve your child in the long run. What *will* serve her, what she *needs* to hear—even if she tells you otherwise and throws it back in your face—is that you love her, no matter what. Then, just love her. Love her no matter what. Tell her this but also hold this energy in your heart and send her your love every time she comes to mind.

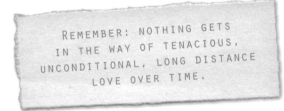

REMEMBER: NOTHING GETS IN THE WAY OF TENACIOUS, UNCONDITIONAL, LONG DISTANCE LOVE OVER TIME.

The more you look after yourself—sort out healthy and unhealthy guilt, perhaps exploring any abandonment or neglect issues in your childhood; adopt the mindset of loving your child no matter what, even if it seems like she doesn't want you (believe me, she does); and treat yourself gently and compassionately—the more you will be able to hold the space of mother to your child within you, come what may. And then, if she becomes ready—which from the experiences of many other mothers apart usually turns out to be 'when' she is ready—you'll be ready and open.

If your child complains about Dad

It's hard to get a balanced view if your child is upset and you only have one side of the story. Your child's age will have a lot of bearing on how you deal will with the problem and, as a rule of thumb, the older she is the more she should be encouraged to resolve it herself—unless the issue is of a serious nature. Supporting your child to find a solution to the problem with her father is the goal.

Whatever your child's age, and whatever the predicament, start by listening carefully. Try to hear your child out without interrupting. Guard against trying to fix the problem. Only ask questions that are relevant to the problem and that are necessary to help you understand, so as to allow your child the opportunity to express herself and get the difficulty out in the open. Having the space to voice her experience will help her to begin to process the problem for herself.

KEEPING YOUR FEELINGS SEPARATE

Listening carefully means that you need to focus fully on your child and not allow what is being expressed to hook in your own pain or guilt. Remember that your aim is to help your child to resolve their difficulty and if your own feelings were to take over or influence whatever your child does next, you wouldn't be serving her best interests. Learning how to communicate a point of view clearly, share a feeling, negotiate a resolution, agree a compromise, are important to your child's development and success in dealing with others. Taking over or allowing your own emotions to dominate will get in the way of this learning.

Observe the reaction inside yourself. If the emotions pull hard within you, feel very strong or remind you of what life was like with your ex or other difficult situations in your life, past or present, you might—if you're not aware of it—react to your child from a place of your own unresolved issues.

> 'She started telling me about how he wouldn't let her out after 9pm and told her to take off her make-up. What she described reminded me of exactly how I used to feel with him—possessed, criticised, controlled. It was hard for me stop myself saying, "I know exactly how you feel, he treated me the same way!"'
>
> *Kathryn*

I realise that experiences such as the example above are capable of bringing back painful or infuriating memories, but when you're sparked by the past, take a deep breath, listen carefully and act with care and consideration. Inappropriate behaviour of one adult partner towards another in a relationship might well be appropriate behaviour for a parent towards a child.

You don't have to be perfect—triggers and unresolved issues abound—but acknowledging a powerful reaction in yourself, recognising that something has been evoked, can be enough to help you separate your own feelings and stop them influencing your child's process in finding a solution. By responding calmly and with empathy you'll avoid creating hostility.

You can't stop your child from feeling difficult or painful feelings but you can help them to find healthy and constructive ways of dealing with them.

There will always be behaviour in others that we find difficult, so try to see any interpersonal problems she might experience as good practice.

Once your child has shared her feelings and you understand the issue, you can help her to find a solution. Try asking questions to facilitate this process:

> *'What could you say to (Dad) to explain your side and how you feel?'*
> *'What do you think (Dad) is concerned or worried about in all this?'*
> *'What would it take (from Dad) for you to agree a solution?'*
> *'What do you think would be a fair compromise?'*
> *'Can you offer any assurances or commitments in exchange for getting what you would like in the situation?'*

Of course, helping your child to find a solution to a problem with their father depends on their age and maturity. Using questions like these could be unrealistic for young children. If your child is very young or if something is really wrong you'll need to talk it over with the adults concerned—your ex and perhaps his new wife.

Being an assertive mother apart also means that you speak up if you have good reason to believe that your children are being abused or neglected. If this is the case, involve the appropriate authorities.

Another reason for approaching the adults directly is when the problem includes adult decisions such as where your child will live, how often you see him or her, where and when they will be picked up or dropped off and so on.

Some final tips for every age and stage

🐾 Provide ongoing reassurance every time you see your child. To maintain trust you need to be truthful in letting her know when change will happen.

🐾 Do your best to remain open so that your child finds it easy to talk to you and allow her time to work through and understand what she feels. Until we discover otherwise there is a tendency to fear feelings—that if they acknowledge them

119

we'll become overwhelmed. We can help by teaching children that feelings come and go, and feeling them provides a healthy release.

- By letting your child know that she is understood, by normalising her feelings and helping her find constructive alternatives to destructive behaviour, you will be providing the support she needs to start coming to terms with your separation and the inner strength she needs to deal with other losses which occur in life.

Chapter 9

The best of times: making the most of contact with your child

Being together

'The time with them is so precious. I tell myself I must make the most of it. My kids say, "Stop taking photos all the time" but I can't help it. I want to catch and keep as much as I can of our time together—my memories keep me going when I don't see them.'

Lana

As mothers apart we make the most of every moment spent with our children. When they are with us we can hardly keep our eyes off them. We watch them closely, absorbing their familiarity and noting even the smallest of changes. Their growth fills us with a combination of delight, pride, loss and longing for what we miss out on. An exquisite mixture of happiness and pain. Bittersweet, intensive mothering.

'She was much too big but she'd still sit on my lap. I didn't care about being squashed. I stroked her hair and face and hugged her until my heart felt like it would burst.'

Kathryn

Even with fairly regular contact emotions can run high: the thrill of planning activities before a child arrives, adjusting to a sometimes far from perfect reality, feeling on a high when a special moment is shared, mulling over every word a child says.

'I have loads of ideas and love planning what we'll do together. I'm so excited that I can't sleep a few nights before they arrive.'

Vickie

The expectation of having happy times, harmony, fun, bonding and healing conversations, the hope of finding out more about a child's life, friends, future aspirations, likes

121

and dislikes make for heady, adrenalin charged contact. And the less contact a mother has the higher and lower the roller coaster ride.

How to make sure your child has a good time when you're together and not lose yourself in the process

At the risk of appearing to pour water on your fireworks, I suggest you take a deep breath and slow down. It's because the stakes are so high for you and your child that I encourage you to take it easy. Your relationship is a marathon run over a lifetime, not 'a make up for lost time' sprint. Slow motion will get you there quicker.

Here are some suggestions for helping to create a sustainable, harmonious relationship with your child.

EMOTIONAL JET LAG

I once heard a divorced Dad say that his children suffered from 'emotional jet lag' when they arrived from his ex-wife's home. Even if your child hasn't taken a flight to be with you it's worth bearing in mind that she will be making a sizable emotional and physical adjustment to acclimatise to life in your home. Hold firm against the pressure inside you wanting to make the most of the precious time—allow your child to 'arrive' at their own speed.

TRY MIRRORING YOUR CHILD'S ENERGY

When you feel the desire to cuddle or have a conversation with your child and it's clear that they don't feel like communicating much, try mirroring their energy level and mood. I'm not suggesting that you become sullen when faced with a moody teenager but if you step out of your urgency to connect with your child and shift your energy to become calm, centred, open and quietly attentive, you will reduce any pressure your child feels to meet your need or pull away from you and allow a more natural and balanced way of interrelating to emerge. Likewise, try being as lively, bouncy and full on as your eight year old and resist your impulse to tell her to calm down (unless it's just before bedtime!). Being an adult and a parent doesn't mean that you can't meet like with like at times.

IT'S OK JUST TO BE TOGETHER

Even though you might feel an urgency to make up for lost time or go out and do lots of things, know that it's OK just to be. There is no rush. If time with your child is limited not rushing becomes even more important. It's in the relaxed, unpressured quiet times that we tend to open up and relate on a deeper level with one another. Take pleasure in everyday situations—cook a meal with your child, listen to music together, curl up and read a book out loud, go for a walk, do a jigsaw. You might laugh at the thought of a jigsaw but they're hard to resist once they're out of the box and their therapeutic value never ceases to amaze me: they bring you physically close to others, they're great for de-stressing, and they provide an element of 'safety' and low levels of intensity when communicating, as eyes can be diverted and fingers are busy.

MAKE ONE-TO-ONE TIME FOR EACH CHILD

If you have more than one child, try to manage the contact you have with them to include individual attention. Having time alone together will keep the special one-to-one relationship between mother and child alive. Days out are helpful but remember that individual interaction can happen in small ways too: reading or discussing an age-relevant book with a child on her own, sending postcards or articles of interest to children separately, having a dance around the living room with one child while the other is having a shower.

THE IMPORTANCE OF SPACE

To help your child feel at home, give them their own space. If you're able to provide them with their own bedroom, great, but if not, having a desk, cupboard or bookcase—somewhere where your child can store their own things, a place where they can be safely left and found again when they return—is important for making them feel like they belong.

THE SIGNIFICANCE OF BEING REAL

Ask your child what they'd like to do, and be honest about what you like doing too. I know you want to give them what they want but bonding and creating togetherness means learning about each other and that means your child discovering more about you too. Being real hasn't anything to do with spending lots of money on activities or presents. Being real isn't competing with their father or feeling inadequate at not being able to compete. It's the work of a lifetime—it can't be forced or hurried and the Skin Horse is able to describe what it really means much better than I.

'Real isn't how you are made,' said the Skin Horse. 'It's a thing that happens to you. When a child loves you for a long, long time, not just to play with, but REALLY loves you, then you become Real.'
'Does it hurt?' asked the Rabbit.
'Sometimes,' said the Skin Horse, for he was always truthful. 'When you are Real you don't mind being hurt.'
'Does it happen all at once, like being wound up,' he asked, 'or bit by bit?'
'It doesn't happen all at once,' said the Skin Horse. 'You become. It takes a long time. That's why it doesn't often happen to people who break easily, or have sharp edges, or who have to be carefully kept. Generally, by the time you are Real, most of your hair has been loved off, and your eyes drop out and you get loose in the joints and very shabby. But these things don't matter at all, because once you are Real you can't be ugly, except to people who don't understand.'

The Velveteen Rabbit—Margery Williams

The need for boundaries and discipline

We want happy days with our child, not rules, discipline and conflict. For mother's apart who have been controlled, bullied or abused within their marriage, the very word 'discipline' can push a button. We left to get away from all of that. Perhaps your ex-partner's version of authority fills you with fear and anger. Maybe you're exploring your newly found freedom and the thought of constraints for you and your child feel like a return to the old order.

But in our hearts we know that children need boundaries and that it's our job as a parent to set them. Structure and routine make children feel more secure. There is a difference between firm, loving boundaries and discipline and heavy handed, retaliatory, inconsistent punishment.

BOUNDARIES

The purpose of setting boundaries is to create a win-win situation and teach our children about the mutual respect, trust and love they will need to grow into mature, understanding adults. Without boundaries, children struggle with their sense of worth and the ability to maintain good relationships. They may have an overdeveloped sense of responsibility, put others' feelings before their own or allow other people to think for them. They may try to control or blame others. They might also allow someone else to define their strengths, weaknesses and abilities. Typical unboundaried behaviour includes: walking into a bedroom without knocking, blaming siblings, interrupting conversations or changing the channel on the TV without checking with others.

BEING A ROLE MODEL

The best way we can teach our children about boundaries is by taking care of our needs, trusting our instincts and valuing ourselves—all the self-care necessities we covered in Chapter 4. Model boundaries for your child; it's one of the best ways for them to learn. You can do this even if you have minimal contact or no contact at all. They might not fully understand how you came to live apart for some years, but your commitment to mutual respect and taking responsibility for your actions will make a difference.

You can role model boundaries for your child by:

- Knowing your own limits.

- Not allowing anyone to violate your physical boundaries.

- Sharing your thoughts and opinions and listening to and accepting thoughts and opinions and life choices in older children, even if they are very different to yours.

- Taking responsibility when things go wrong.

- Standing up for your rights, whether it be taking a faulty item back to the shop or exercising your right to vote.

TIPS FOR SETTING BOUNDARIES

It doesn't matter how much contact you have with your child—you can teach your child about the importance of boundaries for their sake and yours.

- When you notice a boundary needs to be set, do so calmly, firmly and quickly. When you have set a boundary, trust yourself and stick to it.

- Where possible, give your child choices. It's less controlling, they'll learn decision-making skills and with heated issues, it provides face-saving, non-humiliating wiggle room.

- Tell your child what hurts you and what feels good.

- Respect your child's right to privacy including their need for personal space, their relationships with others which are separate from you, their need to speak on the phone in private and so on.

DISCIPLINE

'I find it hard to keep up and bridge the gaps when we don't have contact. It's got harder as they get older. Because I'm not hands-on, day in day out, I don't know what's normal teenage behaviour, or how much their aggression and playing up is because of what they've had to cope with, without me.'

Helen

As mothers apart, we can hang our inability or decision not to discipline our children on a whole host of feelings, failures or skills gaps. We avoid the thorny issue of discipline because of a variety of personal nightmares: guilt, wanting to keep things 'nice', not wanting to be a cruel and horrible mother, fear, not knowing what to do, not wanting to do the wrong thing or make mistakes, trying to protect ourselves from our child's attack ('What right do you have to …'), rejection ('I never want to see you again …'), being an inadequate mother ('Dad's a much better parent than you, at least he understands …')—to name a few.

> AS MUCH AS YOU MIGHT WANT TO AVOID CONFLICT OR DO ANYTHING IN YOUR POWER TO WIN YOUR CHILD OVER, SEPARATION MEANS THAT YOUR CHILD NEEDS CONSISTENCY AND CONTAINMENT NOW MORE THAN EVER BEFORE.

HELP YOURSELF BY …

Learning about children's development and behaviour at different ages, even though parenting books might make you feel guilt and pain. Try an internet search too. It's worth getting to grips with guilt in order to familiarise yourself with what behaviour to expect—it will make the where, when and how to discipline much easier.

WHERE POSSIBLE …

Discuss and maintain communications regarding your child's worrying behaviour with your ex or your child's carer or a professional. Only you will know how realistic this is but challenge yourself before you dismiss the idea. What's more important—your pride and being thought of as not good enough or your child's health, well-being and future happiness?

KNOW THAT WITHOUT A DOUBT …

Loving your child also means saying 'No'.

FIVE DISCIPLINE KEEPSAKES

1. **Keep consistent**

   Don't let inconsistent contact with your child put you off. By keeping your approach to discipline, rules and rewards consistent your child will know where she stands, feel more secure and adjust quicker when she spends time with you.

2. **Keep curious**

   Rather than only focusing on the 'bad' behaviour, try to understand why your child acted inappropriately. Perhaps the acting out is masking a deeper, more serious problem. Looking for hidden clues can also guide you as you teach your child to find more positive and effective ways of dealing with life when it doesn't turn out as hoped.

3. **Keep it simple**

   Have as few rules as possible and stick to them. Chose your absolute non-negotiables carefully and don't weaken. Your child needs to know and feel the limits, so avoid saying 'Alright then, just this once'. Negotiating less crucial, grey areas teaches children communication skills. Offering choices wherever possible avoids loss of face and self-esteem as a consequence.

4. **Keep calm**

   Children can feel a sense of power and enjoyment out of watching you react to a provocation. Remember this is true for parents whether or not they live with their children. Your child will probably be very good at sensing your emotions, vulnerability and guilt hot spots. If you feel yourself losing control, tell your child you're taking some time out. Phone a trusted friend, go for a walk—do whatever it takes to regain perspective.

5. **Keep affirming**

   Living apart from you means your child will lack your attention and might try to get it by behaving badly. Consistent praise and encouragement is far more effective at encouraging good behaviour than paying attention to bad behaviour. Ignoring less serious bad behaviour while highlighting the good might be hard work at first, but it's much more pleasant and beneficial for everyone in the long run.

Being together and apart

Many mothers apart live with one or some of her children and apart from others. If you are one of them, I'm sure you'll experience this as a double-edged sword. Living with a child will bring you joy, boost your confidence and keep you connected to your status as a mother but it can also be a painful daily reminder of the child you live without and heighten any sense of guilt or failure you might feel.

> *'Nothing could have prepared me for how devastated I felt when my third child was born. Just the smell of him made me think of the other two that I hadn't seen in three and a half years. I've never cried so much.'*

Natalie

> *'Two of my children live with us now. My youngest daughter came first and a few months later the second youngest, my second son came. I'm relieved to have them back again but I still miss my other two. Only my husband knows how crushed I am about this. I see my eldest daughter occasionally but my eldest son ignores me.'*

Sara

And there can be rivalry and jealousy between children too:

> *'One minute they would be laughing and playing together and the next fighting viciously. Or we'd be doing something together and if my son, who lives apart from me, thought I was giving my daughter, who lives with me, too much attention he would push her away and say, "Can't you go away and let me do this on my own with Mum, you have her to yourself all the time!"'*

Leah

Other mothers experience such pain at the loss of one child that they can't bring themselves to nurture or play with the other or others. To do so feels like a betrayal of the one they live without.

If you are together and apart from children, you will feel like there is a tug of war going on. Whether it's inside you or whether your children are actually tugging at your emotions, the way to manage is the same:

Love the one you're with.

The child you are with needs your love. Loving her or him doesn't mean that you love the one you're apart from any less.

Big-hearted mothering means that you open up your heart and know within yourself that there is enough love to go

YOU ARE NOT BETRAYING THE CHILD YOU ARE WITHOUT WHEN YOU GIVE LOVE AND ATTENTION TO THE ONE YOU ARE WITH—EVEN IF IT FEELS THAT WAY.

around. You can love deeply from afar and hold the space inside you for the child you live without. Remember, the child you are with lives apart from a sibling. You can help to maintain or establish the relationship between them by making the child who is not with you present. Don't be afraid to bring him or her into conversations: 'I bet Toby would enjoy this, you know how much he loves chocolate', 'I wonder if Katie got caught in all that rain—she has tennis practice on Saturdays'. Involve your child in choosing birthday presents for the absent child and encourage them to speak on the phone or write.

It is possible to love the child you live without as fully and deeply as the child you live with.

Do the work you need to relieve yourself of unnecessary guilt and focus your attention on loving. Aim to be absolutely present with the child in your home and absolutely committed to loving over time and space the child who lives apart from you.

Divide your time the best way you can and reassure your children. Your children need to know that there is enough love to go around and they need to experience it.

It's easy to feel drawn to give extra special attention to the child who lives apart from you but beware.

Even if the child you live with doesn't appear to mind, remember that they will be grappling with a host of mixed emotions which will include guilt, loss, anger and rivalry.

Reassure your children that there is enough love for all of them, verbally and physically, if they bicker. Even if they don't, be mindful of distributing your affection and time evenly. Have quality time alone with each of them, doing something that is of interest to them as an individual. Listen attentively. Affirm and encourage.

Remember to keep things in perspective; sibling rivalry is normal and would have occurred if you all lived together permanently.

Don't tear yourself apart. It's really tough feeling like you're being pulled between children. Above all else, don't trip yourself up by trying to be Supermum. Be attentive and mindful of your children's feelings but don't tear yourself apart trying to create perfection or by feeling their feelings for them. Do your best, then let go.

Being together barometer

Please do this exercise unashamedly and without diminishing your needs. You deserve to have good contact with your child without feeling like you have to suffer, or put up with or give more than you are comfortable with.

You are worthy of first-class self-care. Please understand that being real, centred and in balance is as important for your child as it is for you. *You are your child's role model—teach her how to value herself by valuing yourself.*

Reflect a while on how you feel when you spend time with or have contact with your child.

Write down what comes easily for you, what flows naturally between you—when you feel happy, peaceful, confident and in balance. For example: creating new family traditions with your child, writing and posting a weekly newsletter, learning a new hobby together, phoning after a particular TV programme to have a chat, having as much time outdoors as indoors.

Now write down what is less comfortable. What makes you anxious, less confident, stressed, worn out or depleted? For example: the urge to spend more money than you can afford, saying yes when you want to say no, making allowances for rude or hurtful behaviour, feeling torn between children you live with and without.

What do you need to do less of to ensure that you take care of yourself when you have contact with your child? For example: apologising repeatedly for …, giving automatically without waiting for your child to ask, grumbling about your child's father.

What do you need to do more of to ensure that you take care of yourself when you have contact with your child? Plan good 'aftercare' before a difficult phone call to your child—a treat or a chat, making and taking guiltless 'me' time during visits, explaining a new boundary to your child and making sure everyone sticks to it, writing in your journal.

How are you going to ensure that you take care of yourself and remain in balance from now on? For example: send letters regularly in the spirit of big-hearted mothering—with hope but without expectation, ask a trusted friend to be available for extra tele-phone support during visits, find ways of committing and recommitting yourself to loving deeply over time through affirmations, finding a counsellor and so on.

Being apart

Getting through special days

Birthdays—your child's, your own and those of family members, Mother's Day, religious and public holidays, weddings, christenings and other family gatherings, school plays, sports days, school dances, graduations—the list is endless. Being apart from your child on special days can be some of the loneliest days of your life.

Here are some tips to help you get through special days when you long to be with your child:

- Don't deny or downplay the significance of the day—it is what it is.

- Do send your child a card, letter or present or phone them with a message that comes from your heart—you wish you could be with them, you're thinking of them and you send them love.

- Make the day a conscious one. Treat yourself with extra care and plan to do something that nourishes you if it's a sad day.

- Have a parallel celebration and send your child photos of your day.

- Incorporate a meaningful ritual or symbol into the day to mark the specialness of the occasion. For example, celebrate your child's eighteenth or twenty-first birthday by spending the day with a trusted friend, charting your child's life by talking though how you felt at their birth, looking at old photos, school reports and so on. See if there is anything you'd like to let go of, old letters perhaps, and invite a new, more adult way of relating to your child into your life.

- Congratulate yourself for having such a wonderful child—buy yourself some flowers.

- Write a letter that you never send as a way to process your feelings. Perhaps it's to your child, her father, your father, the legal system—whoever or whatever fits.

- Prepare a 'memory box' (described in the next chapter) that represents the day.

Staying in touch and long distance mothering

Although the distance between you might feel huge, thinking creatively about how you can stay in touch can help you and your child feel like you're bridging the gap.

Phone calls. If you can, arrange a regular time to call. Weekly calls will bring you up-to-date with each other and are frequent enough to encourage sharing of deeper concerns by your child. Consider buying phone cards to send to your child so that they can call when they want to chat. Also consider paying for a phone to be installed in your child's bedroom if you feel this is possible and appropriate.

Mobile phones are another great way to stay in touch, anyplace, any time, and they offer a level of privacy that home phones don't. Text messages are excellent for spontaneous funny, low key, goodnight and I love you moments. Impress your child by using emoticons in texts and e-mails ;o)

The internet offers some exciting ways of staying in touch. It's likely that your child is already very involved so why not join them by making the most of the immediacy of online communication via e-mail accounts and social networking, like MySpace where you can voice chat for free in real time, chat via instant messaging, blog, file share and so on.

Snail mail. It's always exciting receiving post and the sky's the limit when it comes to what you can pop into an envelope or small package. Mail a postcard when you're out for the day, write a number of serialised letters so that your child looks forward to the next instalment, send stickers, the latest collectables, a pressed flower from a walk you went on and anything else that catches your eye.

Here are some other ways of staying connected and letting your child know that you're thinking about them:

- Read the same book as your child and discuss it over the phone

- Sponsor or adopt an animal in your child's name and perhaps visit it too

- Send recordings of your voice, telling your news or reading a story

- Order a personalised, realistic newspaper with your account of your child's recent achievement

- Have a photo of you both made into a puzzle

- Send your child a subscription to their favourite magazine

- Order a personalised music CD—a great idea for very young children as your child's name will be included in the recording

- Send flowers to say well done

- Send chocolate or a teddy bear, just because

- Watch the same TV show and chat about it when you call

- Send teenagers vouchers for a coffee shop or restaurant or cinema tickets

Even though staying in contact might feel painful or it seems like your attempts fall into a black hole—keep at it. More than one mother apart has been amazed to discover that her child has kept letters and cards for years, despite troubled contact.

Chapter 10

Keeping strong when there's no contact

'My girls avoid me in the street, don't take my calls on their mobile phones, ignore text messages and e-mails or, in the case of my elder daughter, sends responses along the lines of "I am too tied up with my life to deal with you. I could but I just don't want to."

'When I left my husband after many years of a wretched marriage he told me very coldly that he would not hesitate to kill me but it would be detected because "inexplicably there are people who are fond of you". He promised to make my life a living hell and said that the first thing he would do was to "get the children". As a loving, caring, professional woman I did not believe that he would ever have any chance of succeeding. My two daughters, who were six and four (I had agonised over the appropriate time—whether to leave the marriage when they were this age rather than bring them up in a hostile environment and leave when they had left school), left with me to go into rented accommodation leaving my ex-husband in the marital home.

'From the start I encouraged a loving relationship between my girls and their Daddy. I sang his praises as a man and a father to such a degree that both girls would ask why I left him. I was uneasy about the bullying and lack of cooperation which underpinned our relationship from day one of my departure. He remarried two months after our divorce and I was delighted as I thought that the animosity would abate. His new wife transpired to be the perfect accomplice and was made to believe that I was a witch who had wrecked his life and that I had spread malicious gossip about her. When I invited her into my home when she was collecting the children she told me that she would never wish to be in the same room as me in front of them. Far from settling down it became open warfare—my girls started to find fault with me and the way we lived. They criticised the lack of funds and that we could not afford a cleaner. My eight year old would go through the larder looking at sell-by dates "as her stepmother had advised". They talked about the lovely family life that their father and stepmother provided for them when they were not with me.

'When my elder daughter was fourteen my-ex husband embarked on legal proceedings to be granted a residence order. Up until this time I had de facto primary care of the girls without there being any need to have it legalised. The well-documented path of Children and Family Court Advisory and Support Service (CAFCASS) officers visiting both homes and interviewing all parties was put in motion. I was faxed by my husband's solicitors at my place of work as I was leaving to collect them from school one Friday in

November 2003 and was informed that I would be prevented from collecting them. In January the following year he was granted a residence order which reversed the arrangement that we had on the grounds that my daughters had chosen not to live with me anymore. I was to see the girls every Wednesday night, staying over, every other weekend and we would divide the school holidays. I pointed out that the court should be suspicious of any application for a residence order in these circumstances. The CAFCASS officer told me that the law states that a fourteen year old is able to make up her own mind where to live and that the wishes of her sister, aged twelve, would be almost equally paramount. I asked for a meeting with senior members of CAFCASS to explain that if they recommended a residence order, and it was granted, I believed that I would be prevented from seeing my children.

'*Three and a half years later I have seen both girls less than a handful of times. I have not returned to the courts as CAFCASS advised I should do "in the unlikely event of Mr X not cooperating" as I do not wish to put my children through the horror of the court process again and they are apparently adamant that this state of affairs is their choice. Communication has been nigh on impossible—the children are alienated from me and each manifests this in very different ways. My ex-husband has shown all the legal correspondence to the girls from a very early age, expressing his anger to them that they are considered by me "not to be mature enough to make up their own minds" and bestowing an inappropriate power to both girls. He has said that my behaviour will cause him to have a heart attack. My elder daughter wrote in abusive tones to say that I would cause the death of her beloved father and if I "called off the lawyers" then she and her sister would see me.*

'*Over the past few years I have had to deal with the ignominy of ringing my elder daughter's new school to discover that they had no record of me as her mother. I produced a solicitor's letter to explain that I had full parental responsibility and, during a meeting with her headmaster and housemistress, learned that my younger daughter had been an inpatient (she attends another school) for several months being treated for anorexia. I had seen my younger daughter a few months earlier and highlighted my concern regarding her severe weight loss and, more tellingly, her demeanour to my ex-husband and his wife, and was told it was "none of my business and to **** off".*

'*The unit responsible for my younger daughter's illness operated a systemic method and I was invited to attend meetings with her and personnel responsible for her care. It was recommended to my ex-husband and his wife that she should be seeing her Mum "who she clearly misses". During sessions with the psychiatrist and social worker, I was told that my daughter had divulged, and asked that I should be told, that "my Mummy is the person I most relate to in my family—she is clever, loving and charismatic, she loves her many friends and they in turn love her", but on hearing this her father threatened to take disciplinary proceedings against the hospital. My troubled, closed down daughter trusted the people who cared for her but this was blown when her father and stepmother told her that they were "bad and wrong to interfere with her feelings about her unfit mother". Despite the pain involved with this process, I was able to be part of my daughter's life when invited to attend these sessions and I also learned the address of where my daughters were living.*

'I did not "leave" my children. We know that no mother ever really does but my girls have been a victim of parental alienation syndrome in the same way as if I had. I always say that I am not a stupid woman. I have had the best City lawyers (paid for by the best friends in the world) but £80,000 later and heading for bankruptcy, I have to date lost my children.'

Lauren

What is parental alienation syndrome?

The term parental alienation syndrome (PAS) was coined in 1985 by Dr Richard A. Gardner, who was a clinical professor of child psychiatry until his death in 2003. Dr Gardner observed and described PAS as a disorder that occurs solely in child-custody disputes in which a child becomes aligned with one parent and preoccupied with the unjustified vilification of the other parent.

Dr Gardner took pains to make clear that PAS isn't the same as brainwashing because it includes the programming by one parent coupled with the child's denigration of the other parent. In severe cases, the child's once loving relationship with the targeted parent is destroyed. He also made clear that PAS does not occur in cases where a parent abuses or neglects a child as the child's hostility towards that parent is justified.

Dr Gardner identified a group of symptoms that usually appear together as a child's action or reactions towards a parent. Children who suffer with moderate or severe PAS will show evidence of most, if not all, of the following symptoms:

- **A campaign of denigration.** This includes the child's own contribution, without guilt, to the 'hatred' of the target parent.

- **Weak, absurd or frivolous rationalisations for the deprecation.** Dr Gardner cites anecdotal examples to explain this symptom, including a boy who said he didn't want to see his father because 'He showed up at the Christmas play and he wasn't supposed to'. This example showed a combination of the child's denigration and the mother's confirmation of the child's rationalisation.

- **Lack of ambivalence.** The child is clear in her belief that the target parent is 'all bad' and the other 'all good'.

- **The 'independent-thinker' phenomenon.** The child says her opinions and requests are her own in a bid to protect the indoctrinating parent, who in turn, says that the child's attitude is completely her own.

- **Reflexive support of the alienating parent in the parental conflict.** Even when both parents are present, the child agrees that the indoctrinating parent is always right and the target parent is always wrong.

- **Absence of guilt over cruelty to and/or exploitation of the alienated parent.** The child doesn't show any love for or appreciation of the target parent, neither does she display any guilt or remorse for this.

- **The presence of borrowed scenarios.** The child demonstrates that she has incorporated the indoctrinating parent's viewpoint as her own. Statements by the child sound rehearsed and as if a wrongdoing by one parent towards another was in fact towards the child herself.

- **Spread of the animosity to the friends and/or extended family of the alienated parent.** PAS spreads to include the extended family and friends who once had positive and loving relationships with the child.

Now, while most experts in the field agree that a child who has been alienated by her parent shares behaviours that reflect Dr Gardner's research and experience, there are very differing opinions on what to call such behaviour and what to do about it. A quick internet search will throw up a baffling array of beliefs on the subject, including whether this behaviour constitutes the medical definition of a syndrome. PAS hasn't as yet been officially recognised as a syndrome by the world standard setter, the US based Diagnostic and Statistical Manual of Mental Disorders (DSM) and, as such, questions about whether it is scientifically proven remain unanswered, along with official recognition in the courts. There are also concerns about misdiagnosis that could result in children who are genuinely fearful of an abusive parent being forced to have contact with him or her.

But as the debate rages on as to whether this type of behaviour is regarded as a syndrome, alienation or aggression, separated parents of both genders who are prohibited from seeing their children and believe they are the victims of an unjust legal system, which issues misguided residency orders and unenforceable contact orders, suffer deeply as a result.

Another mother apart tells her story:

'My problems started when my eight year marriage came to an acrimonious end. The system has failed me but more importantly failed my children. When marriages split there are no support services behind you. I think there needs to be a fundamental change from battling out in court, where one of you ends up the winner and the other the loser—there are simply no winners at the end of the day. Something more supportive and constructive needs to happen before going to court, such as compulsory mediation.

'My ex-husband walked out with my two young children, A and E, then aged four and just under two years old. I went out for the day and I came home to a completely empty house. It was a nightmare. The police were called and my youngest son was returned to me that night but my elder son, who had already at the age of four been "encouraged" to side with my ex-husband, stayed with him. This was on the Saturday and we were in court the following Monday. I made an application to the local county court, and my ex made an application to the high court. Although both courts ruled that the children should be returned to me, he ignored the ruling and did not return the children.

'We then had a six day hearing at the county court which was just the most awful experience, where I felt somebody who didn't know me was starting to make judgements about whether I was a good parent or not. The way the system works, possession is nine-tenths of the law; if you've got the kids from the outset you are in a much stronger position to maintain that status quo, so from the beginning my ex-husband was able to establish a "new normal" with the children, thus initiating the elimination of me as their mother from their lives. At this point my ex-husband used something of the law in his absolute determination to make sure that I didn't have the children—he started making allegations against me that I had hurt the children. There's no criminal level of proof, as you would need in the criminal courts. How do you disprove such allegations? In my case there was no history of him reporting concerns to the GP, no previous issue of social services being called, no reporting of my alleged behaviour to the police—there was nothing to prove that this was happening. It simply wasn't true but he just used this as a weapon against me to "win" the children for himself. He had made it clear from the outset when he took off with the children that he would do "whatever it takes, lie, cheat, steal to make sure you never have the children".

'I was given overnight contact midweek and alternate weekends—an interim residency situation. This is where I feel penalised. I feel my status as a professional working woman wanting to achieve the utopian work–home balance was used against me. My ex-husband was much more flexible with his time as he was running his own business.

'Three years and around fifteen court appearances later, the case got transferred to the high court and a shared residency order was finally granted in October 2003. However, in that time my eldest son had been turned against me. He had been convinced by his

father that I was evil and dangerous and two and half years after the whole proceedings started, he stopped staying with me. My youngest son, E, was staying with me as before but there were constant battles over holiday arrangements where my ex-husband would not be reasonable and agree these with me. Again this is where the system fails; imposing complex contact orders is impossible if one parent won't work cooperatively with the other. We've had child psychiatrists involved and finally a legal guardian was appointed to represent the children at the beginning of 2005. I had been saying since the moment my eldest son was alienated from me that my relationship with my youngest child was at risk. Then, in July 2005, my youngest child also stopped staying. By that stage we had had around forty court appearances and my legal costs were in excess of £70,000.

'A final hearing was held in October 2006 following recommendations from the child psychiatrist and the legal guardian for a Social Services investigation of my ex-husband, as everyone, including the judge, concluded he had caused my sons significant emotional harm. The court did not support this view, however. Instead the judge ruled that the reason my boys did not want to be with me was because, as my ex-husband had alleged, I had hit them and shouted at them. The judge could not conceive that these were lies and refused to believe my explanation that they had been brainwashed against me.

'My ex-husband had been ordered to undergo a psychological assessment by the court. He refused to agree to this unless I did too. To ensure he did, I also agreed to be assessed. My ex-husband again failed to comply with this court order. My assessment concluded that I was a normal, healthy, socially adept, intelligent, robust person who did not show any traits that would suggest that I would hurt my children. The court decided to believe my ex-husband's lies instead of this independent report on me.

'Another appeal through the family courts to be part of my children's lives again is unlikely to be successful and, even if it was, it would not bring my boys back to me. I just have a piece of paper confirming I have shared residency of them, which in reality is not worth the paper it is written on.

'Here we have two children who are my life, who will not even acknowledge me now or talk to me when they see me—they ignore me as if I am a piece of dirt. My ex-husband does nothing to encourage them to do so as any other normal parent would. He believes he has won and that our children, aged eleven and eight and a half, are now old enough to have made up their minds that they don't want me as their mother. This alienation has taken six years and it is absolutely complete now.

'All I have left is to continue to hope and pray that one day when they are old enough and independent enough they will somehow find their way back to me. I will always be waiting for them and my door will always be open. In the meantime I have to survive through this living bereavement, taking one day at a time. There are not many days when I do not a shed a tear over what has happened and how much I miss my boys.

Kissing a photo of them each night is not nearly enough. I miss being involved in their day-to-day lives, sharing their triumphs, being there to support them through their disappointments, giving them hugs and kisses to let them know how much I love them. I write to them regularly and send them weekly text messages. I get no reply. I occasionally see them at school events but they will not talk to me or engage with me in any way. I also have to deal with my ex-husband's constant harassment of the Child Support Agency to pay him child maintenance for my boys—even though I have been excluded from their lives. My ex-husband is not content that he has forced me out of my boys' lives—he wants to destroy me financially as well. I do provide for A and E as best as I can and will continue to do so. At least this way they cannot accuse me of not helping to support them.'

Margaret

How to deal with parental alienation

The degree of anguish and sorrow experienced by mothers apart who are alienated from their children is incomprehensible for most people. It is the stuff of nightmares and I am in awe at the incredible strength of character and the absolute, unfailing commitment of alienated mothers apart, such as the two above. If you are one also, I am so very sorry. I'm sure you don't need me to tell you that there is no easy remedy, that you're almost certainly facing the long haul—and I won't for one moment patronise you with any quick fixes.

The following suggestions are offered with gentleness.

KNOWLEDGE IS POWER: FIND OUT AS MUCH AS POSSIBLE ABOUT PARENTAL ALIENATION

Although understanding more about alienation won't take the pain away, it will help you to get a clearer perspective on your child's behaviour. Your child's rejection and hostility will feel intensely personal but recognising it as one of the symptoms Richard Gardner identified will help you keep things in perspective. Keep abreast of what the medical and legal experts in the field say about PAS by reading the books listed in the resources section (the next edition of DSM will be published in 2011) and searching the internet for papers and newsworthy case studies which might help you make decisions about future legal action.

FIND SUPPORT FROM OTHERS IN A SIMILAR POSITION

You're not alone and sharing the ups, however small, and downs with someone who understands through their own experience can be extremely encouraging. Check the resources section at the end of the book for organisations such as MATCH who will be able to put you in touch with other mothers apart from their children. Parenting forums on the web are an excellent way of reaching out to others. Consider channelling your energy in a positive way by lobbying and campaigning to highlight the issues faced by alienated mothers, fathers and children. Get involved, but be mindful of maintaining balance. It's easy to throw ourselves into causes that touch us personally and reach the core of us. Invest your time but guard against being defined by parental alienation.

RETAIN AS MUCH CONTACT WITH YOUR CHILD AS POSSIBLE

If all contact has fallen away, establishing or maintaining contact with your child's school is a good way of keeping in touch. Speak to the head teacher about your situation and make sure they have your contact details. Request regular communication with your child's teacher about her progress and ask for progress reports to be sent to you. Stay in touch with the school in order to find out about meetings and activities.

Ask a trusted friend or family member to act as a go-between. A third party might be less 'threatening' to your ex and although hearing about your child via someone else might be painful, having information about her welfare and progress, and perhaps even a photo, is better than no news at all.

Do what you can to let your child know that you love and miss them. Consider the symptoms of parental alienation and if you ever have contact, gently remind her of your safe and loving relationship, happy times with grandparents, fun times with friends: 'Do you remember Susie's dog that you used to play with when we lived in Alexander Road? Well, she has a litter of eight beautiful puppies that I'm helping to look after.' Gently tell your child that it's not her job to get involved in matters between you and her father.

Your child will be watching and monitoring your response even though it seems that the focus is on her, and perhaps her hostile behaviour, which leads me to the next point.

AT ALL COSTS, RESIST WHAT WILL PROBABLY BE A STRONG URGE TO ATTACK YOUR EX. ROLE MODEL THE BEHAVIOUR YOU HOPE YOUR CHILD WILL ADOPT. SHOW HER THERE IS ANOTHER WAY.

ANGRY CONTACT

As unpleasant as it is, if your child is antagonistic and aggressive towards you, remind yourself that it is nevertheless a connection. Even if the only thing she has to say to you is how much she hates you, take heart. Hate is not the opposite of love—indifference is. A hateful, hurtful child is demonstrating that she's still very much emotionally connected to you. It might not be the positive, loving connection you want right now but it links you even so.

TRUST YOUR INSTINCTS ON HOW TO CONFRONT ALIENATION

Keep copies of correspondence and write down details of conversations and sequences of events. Find a secure place to keep them. That way they are saved from forgetfulness due to the passing of time and are contained in your home—and more importantly contained in your life. Take advice from the legal profession, speak to others who share similar circumstances but return to yourself, your feelings, your judgement, your intuition on what steps to take. Understand that there's no right way or correct action—you have to do what feels right for you. Take care to come from a place of well-considered action, not *reaction*. Court appeals use your precious energy *and* hard earned money.

TRUST YOUR INSTINCTS ON WHEN YOU SHOULD TAKE A STEP BACK

Understand that you will only take a step back when you are ready. Out of love and concern, your family and friends will, more than likely, start to suggest that you take a break, implore you not to go back to court, try yet again to speak to your ex or his wife, or loiter around the school gates to catch a glimpse of your child. They know you well and despair at witnessing what the strain of your circumstances is doing to you. Chances are high that they will be right in encouraging you to stop. And you will—but only when you are ready. Sadly this will probably be when you are exhausted. When you are ready, reread Chapter 3 on big-hearted mothering over time.

The way forward is to commit to a long-term approach to motherhood—to focus on the lifetime commitment to your children. Nothing will stop you loving your child and you can love deeply, forever, from afar. When you are ready, and with practice, you will learn how to manage the perfectly understandable panic and intensity you feel inside and adopt a place of holding and waiting instead. Finally, I've included the most important action you need to take in the section, 'Take outrageously good care of yourself' below. Please read on. I hope you find some of the other suggestions of use to you too.

Other reasons for no contact

Perhaps you don't have contact with your child for a reason other than parental alienation syndrome. Sometimes unfortunate circumstances, missed opportunities, too much guilt or shame, a lack of understanding by others or life throwing too much at you at one time, leads to a loss of contact or an obstructed contact which feels too hard to bridge. However you have come to lose all contact, the following is written for you.

TAKE OUTRAGEOUSLY GOOD CARE OF YOURSELF

If you've been battling against systems or institutions, come head to head with authorities or procedures, or have otherwise had your character and ability to mother called to account, it's highly likely that your self-esteem has taken a battering and that your self-worth is at rock bottom.

> YOUR NUMBER ONE PRIORITY, ABSOLUTELY AND WITHOUT QUESTION, HAS TO BE YOU.

Things to remind yourself of:

- No one who is prevented from seeing their child or who longs to see their child and cannot will remain untouched by the trauma of this loss.

- Profound grief, upset and anger are normal reactions to this situation. It's important for you to express and have an outlet for your feelings. Don't let anger turn into depression. If you feel overwhelmed, a prolonged sense of hopelessness or mood swings, have difficulty sleeping, increase your use of alcohol or drugs or have any physical symptoms—find the support you need. Ask a trusted friend to help you find the right person, if necessary.

Make sure you eat healthily and get enough sleep. Practise extremely good self-care on special days, as they are bound to be particularly difficult for you. Reread the tips under 'Getting though Special Days' in Chapter 9.

CREATE A MEMORY BOX

A memory box is a personalised container for the safekeeping of items that represent the unique relationship between you and your child. The creation of the box itself can be a healing process and symbolise hope for the future. Choose a solid box and decorate it using craft materials, photos, stickers, ribbons, flowers or simply paint it any way you like that gives you pleasure. Decorate and line the inside too. Choose items that have special significance to you and your child, but keep it a hopeful, happy place. It might contain baby items from the past along with things you collect as you live your life.

The idea is that it charts a journey of experiences and memories that can be shared with your child at a later date. The contents will help you fill the gaps of the time you spent apart and give your child a good idea of your personality, interests, hobbies—things that are important to you. You might include a lock of hair, poems written by you or others, photos, voice recordings of grandparents, videos of special occasions, pressed wild flowers from a walk through the woods, shells and pebbles from a sunny day at the beach, sketches, watercolours—the list is endless. Have fun—make your memory box an expression of you.

COMPILE A MEMORY BOOK

A memory book or a scrapbook has the same purpose as the memory box. It's a log, in a diary format if you prefer, of memorable days and happy 'just because' days. Write about life, funny stories in the news, jokes, special days and spontaneous moments. Write how you feel, where you went, what you saw, who went with you—alongside memories of your child as a baby. Include anything you are moved to write, but keep it positive. Draw pictures, doodle, paint, stick photos and pictures alongside captions and word bubbles. Think about sharing the snapshots and details of what you include with your child at some point in the future. Be creative, express yourself.

NEVER GIVE UP HOPE

With the deepest respect for all that you have endured, I say never give up hope. At the risk of sounding like I'm minimising your struggle and pain (please know that I'm not)—I say, you never know what's around the corner. Stories abound of children's natural curiosity to find out about the parent they've been separated from for all sorts of reasons. I don't for one moment want to make you feel you ought to be thankful for your lack of contact, but your child knowing little about you or having a father that bad-mouthed you can create a greater curiosity, a greater tension and even a degree of rebellion that could propel your child to your door.

Bide your time. Live as well and as fully as you can, one day at a time, respecting your child's right to learn about life in her own time and pace. Don't let your urgency force your child into anything she's not ready for. If it's appropriate, send letters, text messages or try to phone. Wait patiently and lovingly, and read the next chapter too.

Chapter 11

A mother apart over time

'We can grieve and grieve hard, and come out of it tear-stained, rather than shame-stained. We can come out deepened, fully acknowledged, and filled with new life ... Although there will be scars and plenty of them, it is good to remember that in tensile strength and ability to absorb pressure, a scar is stronger than skin.'

Women Who Run With the Wolves —Clarissa Pinkola Estés

The strength of scar tissue

As mothers apart we are strong. Sometimes it takes a while for us to discover this, especially if we've been told by others that we're weak, a failure, useless, stupid, gullible, selfish for focusing on our career, foolish for finding love and tenderness, overemotional, hypersensitive, getting too big for our boots or any other 'get back into your box' message.

It is true that we have a particularly painful path to walk. But as we learn big-hearted mothering we broaden and deepen our capacity to love, open ourselves to face our pain and guilt instead of blocking it or running from it. We understand that resistance narrows and closes down possibilities and so, with the passing of time, we become tenacious, big-hearted mothers who are able to let go and hold on in equal measure—even though it feels like our heart is breaking. Indeed, many of us know how it feels to have our heart broken, sometimes over and over again. And as we learn to keep an open heart, we learn acceptance of ourselves, our lives and the decisions we made. We discover that we have more room to live and be and gradually find inner peace, acceptance and serenity. We are able to love others more deeply and, most importantly, to love ourselves.

Over the years, I have found hope and inspiration in many big-hearted mothers apart who have amazing stamina and dignified presence in equal measure. Strong women with many scars who are living proof that 'in tensile strength and ability to absorb pressure, a scar is stronger than skin'.

'I never knew I was so strong. In a funny way all the hardships, living apart from my children, have made me more determined to make the most of my life.'

Debbie

As our children grow up

I understand that if your child is very young, the thought of having to wait until she is a young adult before you have the relationship you want with her feels unbearable. If this is true for you, it's my dearest wish that the resolution you long for happens soon.

There is a strange contradiction in life which is that most things take longer than you think to come to fruition and yet they come upon you quicker than you imagine, often feeling quite sudden. 'It only seems like yesterday that he was a babe in arms!' cries the mother of the twenty-eight-year-old bridegroom. His friends think she's crazy but mothers of grown children the world over would nod their heads with understanding and empathy.

Over time and quite suddenly children grow up, start to question, challenge and think things through for themselves. This is true for all children, whether brought up by one parent or both. The point at which your child starts to think for herself will depend on who she is as an individual and the circumstances of your separation. Growing up is a bewildering process. The teenage years are a time of self-focus, hormones, experimenting in the world and, above all, they're about learning to stand on our own two feet—becoming oneself rather than being a parent's child. This could mean that your child is more likely to contact you as she seeks to separate from the parent she lives with. On the other hand, both parents could become a 'no go' area. Remember that teenagers need to separate from their parents and in doing so will often say and do things they know will upset you.

I can't promise you the relationship you hope for with your child. What I do know is that growing up includes starting to think autonomously and questioning the status quo. And children become curious about absent parents.

Sometimes, especially when parental alienation has been severe, children have a lot of distortion and confusion that can take years to work through. I won't kid you by saying that a happy reunion is just around the corner. What I will say is:

🐾 What children hold on to and remember about a loving relationship often comes as a surprise to mothers apart years later.

🐚 An adult child becoming a parent can be a catalyst for reconnection and understanding.

🐚 Remember that anger directed at you is still contact, even though it's not the type you'd like from your child or adult child.

'One of my twins was very angry for a very long time and even in adulthood has, I think, kept some of his fury about the whole break-up, though recently this seems to be waning, mercifully. Meanwhile my daughter and I have an amazing relationship (which has been pretty good ever since she reached her later teens) and continue in frequent, almost constant, touch even though she lives on the other side of the world. She has two children of her own and visits England regularly each year, while I am usually able to go out and visit her during the winter—which is wonderful from every point of view.'

Natasha

Love and healing

'My daughter might be estranged from me but those feelings of love that I have for her no one can ever take away from me, and that makes me feel better and good, that I always have and always will love her.'

Carla

The attitude of this mother apart says it all. No one can stop you from loving. No matter what others say about you—how you might be misunderstood, have your character deformed or exposed in court, even if you are confused and don't really know how or why you became separated from your child—your love stands valid and true.

Trying to be the perfect mother splits us from our true selves. Being a good enough mother liberates us to be ourselves. Being true to yourself is one of the greatest lessons we can role model for our children. Being loved for who we are is what we all yearn for. Love yourself for being the good enough mother that you are, and love your child for being who they are—whether they are miles away or just around the corner, even if they behave appallingly towards you and tell you that they hate you or you have ruined their life. Just love them.

Loving deeply requires that you make yourself vulnerable—and I urge you to risk, open your heart and love. We are healed through love and loving. You'll know this to be true because you'll feel like the mother apart above when she says 'that makes me feel better and good, that I always have and always will love her'.

Keeping the door open

For some of us there is sudden change.

'I wouldn't have believed it was possible, that anything would change, but it did. It all changed quite suddenly in the end and my son came to live with me. I feel very lucky but I would say to all Mums apart from their children, never give up hope of being reunited.'

Shannon

Along with your heart, keep your door open. Anything can happen at any time, and it does. Find the place of balance within you—a place which holds the possibility for a reversal of the status quo, while living life to the full at the same time. Tricky? At first it is but with practice and, in time like the Chi Kung master finding the balance of yin (thinking and spirit) and yang (physical body) you will find your place of inner balance, and the pain within will ease. Being human we lose our centre with the ups and downs of what life throws at us, but don't let that put you off. Just focus on balancing yourself again. The more you practice the easier it will become to return to a place of acceptance and serenity within yourself.

For many of us, mothering apart means a journey lasting many years in which change is incremental, and with numerous peaks and troughs along the way. Even so, the principles of keeping an open heart and open door still apply—as the mother apart below describes so well—and it's this ending and beginning I'll leave you with, along with my final wish for your journey: May you live a full and peaceful life, with much learning, love and laughter along the way.

'I mentioned to my nineteen-year-old daughter that I was going to Israel. "I'll come", she said. We stayed with family, confined together in a room for the first time in five years, but how would we get on after such a time apart?

'Years earlier, she'd left as a squabbling angry, rebellious teenager saying it was easier to live with her father and sister than me—a hysterical, screaming mother trying to get her to do homework to achieve good grades. My ex-husband sympathised that she could not live with her "mad" mother.

'The Israel experience was not easy. The first night she burst into tears: "I hate you. I hate my job. I hate London. You and Dad are as bad as each other." The tirade continued. I never slept.

'The next morning the sun shone, the sea shimmered and my daughter seemed a little less angry. I kept a distance. We spent the day together but sometimes apart. Sometime she called me "Mum", other times she didn't.

'We became friends for a while, then something was said and the terrible rage returned: "You're always criticising Dad, you do it all the time." I remained impassive, silent. After all, I'd been divorced from her father for ten years.

'The week went on. She laughed at silly things I did, getting to know my new digital camera. I asked for help in using it properly. One evening she walked off in a strop. I tried to find her, then heard a shrill voice calling "Mum". She hadn't gone far.

'On our return I offered to pay for a cab to take her back to her Dad's. "It's easier for me to come back to you," she said. I gave her a lift back the following night. "Would you go on holiday with your Mum again?" I asked. She laughed. "I'll send you the keys to the house—you can come and go as you please.""Okay", she said.'

Additional sources of help and advice

Find a counsellor

This book draws on counselling and psychotherapy insights and techniques to offer you gentle, self-exploratory exercises. All exercises are explained fully and apart from one or two that suggest that you share your feelings with a trusted friend, they can be completed on your own, in your own time.

It is part of being human to experience highs and lows and there are times when all of us feel vulnerable, whether or not we live apart from our child. However, if feelings of deep depression, acute pain or anxiety seem to be growing out of proportion and are affecting your daily life, you need to consider professional help. If feelings of life not being worth living, prolonged sleep disturbance, bouts of crying, overwhelming feelings of hopelessness or despair become an everyday occurrence, please don't ignore them. Sometimes physical symptoms, such as insomnia, excessive tiredness or headaches, may indicate something is psychologically wrong.

Opening up to friends or family about your feelings can help but, surprisingly, it can be easier to talk to a stranger about things. A good counsellor or psychotherapist can help you explore thoughts and feelings in an honest, confidential and non-judgemental environment.

So how do you find that special someone to talk to? Please visit my website www.sarahhart.co.uk to find out about the counselling I offer. The British Association for Counselling and Psychotherapy (BACP) also has a list of trained therapists in all areas of the United Kingdom. Your GP may have a counsellor attached to the practice or may be able to make a referral. It's important to find someone who understands and has empathy for women's issues, loss and separation. Use your instincts and take time to find a therapist who you can trust and open your heart to.

The organisations below offer a range of related support:

MATCH (Mothers Apart from Their Children)
  BM Box 6334
  London
  WC1N 3XX (send sae)
  www.matchmothers.org

MATCH is a nationwide self-help group for women living apart from their children, offering unconditional and non-judgemental understanding, support and friendship. MATCH was registered as a charity in 2006 after twenty-eight years as a self-help group.

Childline

Childline is the free helpline for children and young people in the UK. Children and young people can call on 0800 1111 to talk about any problem, twenty-four hours a day, or visit

www.childline.org.uk

The Equal Parenting Council

www.equalparenting.org

The Equal Parenting Council campaigns to keep children in touch with their parents after divorce and separation.

Families Need Fathers (FNF)

134 Curtain Road
London
EC2A 3AR
Helpline: 0870 760 7496
www.fnf.org.uk

FNF is a charity providing support to divorced and separated parents on shared parenting issues arising from family breakdown.

Grandparents Association

Moot House
The Stow
Harlow
Essex
CM20 3AG
Helpline: 0845 434 9585
www.grandparents-association.org.uk

The Grandparents Association's first aim is to promote full participation by grandparents to ensure that contact is maintained between grandparents and their grandchildren when the family unit breaks down or there is conflict.

It's Not Your Fault

www.itsnotyourfault.org

This website offers practical information for children, young people and parents going through a family break-up.

JUMP (Jewish Unity for Multiple Parenting)

020 8386 6282

www.jump-parenting.co.uk

JUMP is a voluntary Jewish support and lobby group that supports non-resident parents and their children after divorce and separation.

NCH (National Children's Home)

85 Highbury Park

London

N5 1UD

020 7704 7000

www.nch.org.uk

NCH was founded in 1869 and known for many years as the National Children's Home. As one of the UK's leading children's charities, it is now known as NCH, the children's charity, and helps children achieve their full potential through various services.

National Family Mediation (NFM)

7 The Close

Exeter

Devon

EX1 1EZ

01392 271610

www.nfm.org.uk

NFM is a network of local not-for-profit family mediation services in England and Wales which offers help to couples, married or unmarried, who are in the process of separation and divorce.

For information about services in Scotland call 0131 5589898 or visit

www.familymediationscotland.org.uk

Parentline Plus

520 Highgate Studios

53–79 Highgate Road

Kentish Town

London

NW5 1TL

0800 800 2222
www.parentlineplus.org.uk

Parentline Plus offer a range of services including a free, twenty-four hour phone line for any issues connected to parenting, parenting groups and workshops, plus e-mail and text support.

Resolution – first for family law
(used to be the Solicitors Family Law Association)
www.resolution.org.uk

Resolution is an organisation of over 5,000 solicitors who are committed to promoting a non-confrontational atmosphere for family law matters.

Reunite
PO box 7124
Leicester
LE1 7XX
Advice line: 0116 2556 234
www.reunite.org

Reunite is the leading UK charity specialising in international parental child abduction.

Women's Aid
Women's Aid
PO Box Bristol 291
BS99 7WS
Freephone twenty-four hour national domestic violence helpline: 0808 200 0247
www.womensaid.org.uk

Women's Aid is the key national charity working to end domestic violence against women and children.

MENTAL HEALTH SERVICES

Advice and help for bipolar disorder, depression and postnatal depression can be received from the following organisations, amongst others:

Depression Alliance
212 Spitfire Studios
63–71 Collier Street
London

N1 9BE
0845 123 2320
www.depressionalliance.org

Depression Alliance is the leading UK charity for people affected by depression.

MDF The Bipolar Organisation
Castle Works
21 St George's Road
London
SE1 6ES
0845 634 0540
www.mdf.org.uk

MDF The Bipolar Organisation is a user-led charity working to enable people affected by bipolar disorder (manic depression) to take control of their lives.

Mind
15–19 Broadway
London
E15 4BQ
Information line: 0845 766 0163
www.mind.org.uk

Mind is the leading mental health charity in England and Wales.

The Royal College of Psychiatrists
National Headquarters
17 Belgrave Square
London
SW1X 8PG
020 7235 2351
www.rcpsyh.ac.uk

The Royal College of Psychiatrists is the professional and educational body for psychiatrists in the United Kingdom and the Republic of Ireland.

Bibliography and further reading

FURTHER READING

Cross, Penny, *Lost Children: A Guide for Separating Parents*, Velvet Glove Publishing, 2000

CHAPTER 1

Estés, Clarissa Pinkola, *Women Who Run With the Wolves: Contacting the Power of the Wild Woman*, Rider, 1992

Geraghty, Anne, *In the Dark and Still Moving*, The Tenth Bull, 2007

Gustafson, Diana L., *Unbecoming Mothers: The Social Production of Maternal Absence*, Haworth Clinical Practice Press, 2005

Jackson, Rosie, *Mothers Who Leave: Behind the Myth of Women Without Their Children*, Harper Collins, 1994

Stewart, Susan, 'Nonresisdent Mothers' and Fathers' Social Contact with Children', *Journal of Marriage and the Family*, 61(4), 894–907

CHAPTER 3

Doka, Kenneth, *Disenfranchised Grief: Recognizing Hidden Sorrow*, Jossey-Bass Inc., 1999

Kübler-Ross, Elisabeth, *On Death and Dying*, Simon & Schuster, reprint edition 1997 please visit www.elizabethkubler.com and www.ekrfoundation.org

CHAPTER 4

Carroll, Lewis, *Through the Looking Glass*, Penguin Books, new edition 1994

Lerner, Harriet, *The Dance of Anger: A Woman's Guide to Changing the Pattern of Intimate Relationships*, Element, 2004

Lindenfield, Gael, *Self Esteem: Simple Steps to Develop Self Worth and Heal Emotional Wounds*, Element, 2000

Massey, Alexandra, *Beat Depression and Reclaim Your Life*, Virgin Books, 2005

Scott, Susan, *Fierce Conversations: Achieving Success in Work and in Life, One Conversation at a Time*, Piatkus, 2002

CHAPTER 5

Bancroft, Lundy, *Why Does He Do That? Inside the Minds of Angry and Controlling Men*, Berkley Publishing Group, 2003

Bower, Sharon and Bower, Gordon, *Asserting Yourself: A Practical Guide for Positive Change*, Perseus Books, 1991

Engel, Beverley, *The Emotionally Abused Woman: Overcoming Destructive Patterns and Reclaiming Yourself*, Fawcett Books, 1992

Persaud, Raj, *The Mind: A User's Guide*, Transworld Publications, 2007

Redfield Jamison, Kay, *An Unquiet Mind*, Picador, 1997

CHAPTER 6

Gibran, Khalil, *The Prophet*, Pan Books, 1991

CHAPTER 7

Geraghty, Anne, *How Loving Relationships Work: Understanding Love's Living Force*, Vega, 2003

CHAPTER 8

Beveridge, J. and Bradley, A., *How to Help Your Children Survive Your Divorce*, Foulsham, 2004

Bowlby, John, *Attachment and Loss*, Pimlico, new edition 1997

Davenport, G. C., *An Introduction to Child Development*, Collins Educational, 1994

Doane, Janice and Hodges, Devon L., *From Klein to Kristeva: Psychoanalytical Feminism and the Search for the Good Enough Mother (Critical Perspectives on Women and Gender)*, University of Michigan Press, 1992

Estés, Clarissa Pinkola, *Women Who Run With the Wolves: Contacting the Power of the Wild Woman*, Rider, 1992

Harlow, H. F. and Harlow, M. K., 'Effects of Various Mother-Infant Relationships on Rhesus Monkey Behaviors', in B. M. Foss (ed.) *Determinants of Infant Behavior* (Vol. 4), Methuen, 1969

Maclean, Mavis, *Together and Apart: Children and Parents Experiencing Separation and Divorce*, Joseph Rowntree Foundation, 2004

Smith, P., Cowie, H. and Blades, M., *Understanding Children's Development*, Blackwell, 2003

BOOKS ON DIVORCE FOR CHILDREN

Blume, Judy, *It's Not the End of the World*, Macmillan Children's Books, 1998 (9–13 years)

Brown, L. and Brown, M., *Dinosaurs Divorce: A Guide for Changing Families*, Little, Brown and Company, 1986 (5–8 years)

Cole, Babette, *Two of Everything*, Red Fox, new edition 2000 (4–8 years)

Lansky, Vicki, *It's Not Your Fault, Koko Bear: A Read-Together Book for Parents and Young Children During Divorce*, Book Peddlers, 1998 (3–7 years)

Levins, Sandra, *Was It the Chocolate Pudding? A Story for Little Kids About Divorce*, Magin ation Press (American Psychological Association), 2005 (2–6 years, a story about Mum leaving home, with 'Note to Parents' by a psychologist)

Wilson, Jacqueline, *The Suitcase Kid*, Corgi Yearling Books, 2006 (9–13 years)

CHAPTER 9

Williams, Margery, *The Velveteen Rabbit or How Toys Become Real*, Running Press, 1998

CHAPTER 10

Gardner, Richard A., *The Parental Alienation Syndrome*, Creative Therapeutics, Inc., 1998

CHAPTER 11

Estés, Clarissa Pinkola, *Women Who Run With the Wolves: Contacting the Power of the Wild Woman*, Rider, 1992

Index